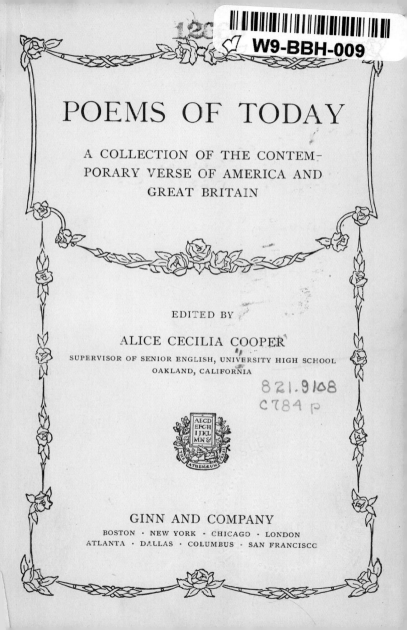

POEMS OF TODAY

A COLLECTION OF THE CONTEM-
PORARY VERSE OF AMERICA AND
GREAT BRITAIN

EDITED BY

ALICE CECILIA COOPER

SUPERVISOR OF SENIOR ENGLISH, UNIVERSITY HIGH SCHOOL
OAKLAND, CALIFORNIA

GINN AND COMPANY

BOSTON · NEW YORK · CHICAGO · LONDON
ATLANTA · DALLAS · COLUMBUS · SAN FRANCISCO

E.S. Melear

5-2-44 mbr

1·26·45·gfw

The Athenæum Press

GINN AND COMPANY · PRO-
PRIETORS · BOSTON · U.S.A.

PREFACE

The poems collected in this volume have been chosen with a single aim,—to give students a happy introduction to the poetry of the first quarter of this century.

Without question much of the poetry of today is beautiful and worthy, and will make its own way with younger readers if it is presented to them through verse which is within their reach and interests. Clearly, if they are to enjoy it, they must understand it and find in it a message for themselves.

Since poetry, and not the poets, is the theme of the collection, the sequence of the volume has been arranged to show the contribution which poetry makes to the widening aspects of life. This cumulative arrangement, both within each section and of the sections themselves, will, it is believed, lead the student naturally from an initial enjoyment of melody and theme to the beginnings of an appreciation of poetic expression and vision.

Since to foster a real enjoyment of contemporary poetry is the primary aim of the volume, the editorial equipment has been kept to a minimum, and what has been included—brief biographical notes, a simple discussion of poetic forms, and suggestive study helps for the teacher's use—will, it is hoped, contribute directly to that aim.

If "Poems of Today" serves to stimulate an interest in modern verse, it will have served well its purpose as a guide to the broad highway of poetry.

ALICE C. COOPER

ACKNOWLEDGMENTS

The editor acknowledges with thanks the courtesy of the following publishers in granting permission to reprint poems from their copyrighted publications:

Messrs. D. Appleton and Company. Poems from Henry Newbolt and Frank L. Stanton.

The Bobbs-Merrill Company. Poems from James Whitcomb Riley.

Brentano's. Poems from Harry Kemp and Francis Ledwidge.

Jonathan Cape. Poems from William H. Davies.

Dodd, Mead & Company. Poems from Rupert Brooke, Austin Dobson, Fannie Stearns Davis Gifford, and Marjorie L. C. Pickthall.

George H. Doran Company. Poems from Berton Braley, Amelia Josephine Burr, Joyce Kilmer, Christopher Morley, John Oxenham, and Cicely Fox Smith.

Doubleday, Page & Company, and A. P. Watt and Company. Poems from Rudyard Kipling.

E. P. Dutton & Company. Poems from Helen Gray Cone; Winifred M. Letts ("Spires of Oxford").

Harcourt, Brace and Company, Inc. Poem from Thomas A. Daly.

Harper & Brothers. Poems from Dana Burnet, Guy Wetmore Carryl, and Arthur Guiterman.

Henry Holt and Company. Poems from Sarah N. Cleghorn, Walter de la Mare, Robert Frost, Carl Sandburg, and Margaret Widdemer.

Houghton Mifflin Company. Poems from Herbert Bashford, William Aspenwall Bradley, Anna Hempstead Branch, Abbie Farwell Brown, Florence Earle Coates, John Drinkwater, Richard Watson Gilder, Louise Imogen Guiney, Amy Lowell, Alice Freeman Palmer, Josephine Preston Peabody, Robert Haven Schauffler, and Frank Dempster Sherman.

Mitchell Kennerley. Poems from Florence Kiper Frank, Edna St. Vincent Millay, and Shaemas O'Sheel.

John Lane Company. Poems from Rupert Brooke and Angela Morgan.

Little, Brown & Company. Poems from Denis A. McCarthy.

Lothrop, Lee & Shepard Co. Poems from Sam Walter Foss and Richard Burton.

David McKay, Philadelphia. Winifred M. Letts ("In Service" in "Songs from Leinster").

Macmillan and Company, Ltd., London. Poems from Alfred Austin and Thomas Hardy.

Thomas Bird Mosher. Poems from Thomas S. Jones, Jr., Lizette W. Reese, and Edith M. Thomas.

Princeton University Press. Poem from John Stoltze.

The Reilly and Lee Company. Poem from Edgar A. Guest.

Charles Scribner's Sons. Poems from William E. Henley, Corinne R. Robinson, Edwin Arlington Robinson, Alan Seeger, Henry van Dyke, and John Hall Wheelock.

Martin Secker. Poem from James Elroy Flecker.

Small, Maynard and Company. Poems from Richard Hovey; Laurence Housman; and Madison Cawein ("The Old Home").

Frederick A. Stokes Company. Poems from Alfred Noyes.

Yale University Press. Poems from Karle Wilson Baker, William Rose Benét, James Fenimore Cooper, Jr., and William Alexander Percy.

The following magazines and newspapers have also graciously given permission to include verse from their copyrighted publications:

American Lumberman. Poem from Douglas Malloch.

Boston Evening Transcript. Poems from Edwin Francis Edgett and Louella C. Poole.

Farm, Stock, and Home. Poem from Hugh J. Hughes.

New Republic. Poem from Joseph Auslander.

New York Sun. Poem from Minnie Leona Upton.

Poetry: A Magazine of Verse. Poems from Nancy Campbell, Louise Driscoll, Helen Hoyt, and Lady Leonora Speyer.

The Step Ladder. Poem from Harry Noyes Pratt.

Youth's Companion. Poem from Nancy Byrd Turner.

The editor takes further pleasure in acknowledging her indebtedness to and in thanking the following authors for their personal permission to include their poems:

John Stanhope Arkwright, Joseph Auslander, Karle Wilson Baker, Herbert Bashford, Professor Katharine Lee Bates, William Rose Benét, Laurence Binyon, Francis W. Bourdillon (through Mrs. F. W. Bourdillon), William Aspenwall Bradley, Berton Braley, Anna Hempstead Branch, Dr. Robert Bridges, Abbie Farwell Brown, John Buchan, Dana Burnet, Amelia Josephine Burr, Dr. Richard Burton, Nancy Campbell, Bliss Carman, John Vance Cheney, Gilbert K. Chesterton, Samuel T. Clover, Florence Earle Coates, Helen Gray Cone, Ina Donna Coolbrith, Charlotte Holmes Crawford, Mary Carolyn Davies, Walter de la Mare, Dr. James Main Dixon, John Drinkwater, Louise Driscoll, Edwin Francis Edgett, Captain David Fallon, Dr. John Finley, Jeanne Robert Foster, Lieutenant-Colonel William Campbell Galbraith, Hamlin Garland, Wilfrid Wilson Gibson, Eva Gore-Booth, Gerald Gould, Agnes K. Gray, Sarah P. McL. Greene, Arthur Guiterman, Hermann Hagedorn, Thomas Hardy, Ella Higginson, Professor Alfred E. Housman, Helen Hoyt (Mrs. Jack Lyman), Rupert Hughes, Wallace Irwin, Richard Le Gallienne, Robert Loveman, Amy Lowell, Edwin Markham, John Steven McGroarty, Lloyd Mifflin (through Dr. Houston Mifflin), Christopher Morley, Alfred Noyes, John Oxenham, Albert Bigelow Paine, Alice Freeman Palmer (through Professor George H. Palmer), Josephine Preston Peabody (Mrs. Lionel Marks), Samuel Minturn Peck, Eden Phillpotts, Louella C. Poole (Mrs. Julius Pähtz), Arthur Powell, Canon Hardwicke Drummond Rawnsley (through Mrs. H. D. Rawnsley), Jessie B. Rittenhouse, James Logie Robertson, Edwin Arlington Robinson, Professor George Santayana, Robert Haven Schauffler, Professor Clinton Scollard, Lady Leonora Speyer, Sara Teasdale (Mrs. Ernst B. Filsinger), Edith M. Thomas, Charles Hanson Towne, Nancy Byrd Turner, Katharine Tynan (Mrs. Henry Hinkson), Louis Untermeyer, Reverend Howard Arnold Walter (through Mr. H. S. Walter), John Hall Wheelock, Marguerite Wilkinson (Mrs. James G. Wilkinson), and Reverend Charles Coke Woods.

CONTENTS

CONTENTS

PAGE

PLACES AND PERSONS

CONTENTS

CONTENTS

"THE EARTH'S UNCEASING MELODY"

INTRODUCTORY POEM

"TELL ME, WHAT IS POETRY—"

Jeanne Robert Foster

Tell me, what is poetry—
Wind in the pines along the sea,
Wind in the forest-browned lanes of sedge,
Lying close to the sand's white edge;
Song of the wave and the muttering roar
Of breakers lashing a wintry shore,
Tinkling sounds where waters slip
Through blue sea caves, drip by drip.

Tell me, what is poetry—
The earth's unceasing melody;
Dawn song, night song, birds awhir,
Fields where the bee is worshiper;
Drowsy drone of the summer rain,
Chirruping calls from ripening grain,
Cicada, cricket, shrilling low;
Nature's music in ebb and flow.

Tell me, what is poetry—
The heart's undying ecstasy,
Songs of our faith, our hopes, our tears,
Songs of the joys of passing years,
Laughter of children, glory of spring,
Tenderness for each blind dumb thing;
Praise when we bend 'neath the chastening rod;
Music that leads us up to God.

POEMS OF TODAY

PATRIOTISM AND HEROISM

"VIVE—LA—FRANCE!". (PAGE 24)

AMERICA THE BEAUTIFUL

Katharine Lee Bates

O beautiful for spacious skies,
  For amber waves of grain,
For purple mountain majesties
  Above the fruited plain!
    America! America!
  God shed His grace on thee,
And crown thy good with brotherhood
  From sea to shining sea!

O beautiful for pilgrim feet,
  Whose stern, impassioned stress
A thoroughfare for freedom beat
  Across the wilderness!
    America! America!
  God mend thine every flaw,
Confirm thy soul in self-control,
  Thy liberty in law!

O beautiful for heroes proved
  In liberating strife,
Who more than self their country loved,
  And mercy more than life!
    America! America!
  May God thy gold refine,
Till all success be nobleness,
  And every gain divine!

3

O beautiful for patriot dream
  That sees beyond the years
Thine alabaster cities gleam
  Undimmed by human tears!
    America! America!
  God shed His grace on thee,
And crown thy good with brotherhood
  From sea to shining sea!

A TOAST TO THE FLAG

JOHN DALY

Here's to the Red of it!
There's not a thread of it,
No, nor a shred of it,
In all the spread of it
  From foot to head,
But heroes bled for it,
Faced steel and lead for it,
Precious blood shed for it,
  Bathing it Red.

Here's to the White of it!
Thrilled by the sight of it,
Who knows the right of it,
But feels the might of it,
  Through day and night.
Womanhood's care of it
Made manhood's dare for it;
Purity's prayer for it
  Keeps it so White.

Here's to the Blue of it!
Heavenly view of it,
Star-spangled hue of it,
Honesty's due of it,
    Constant and true.
Here's to the whole of it,
Stars, stripes, and pole of it,
Here's to the Soul of it,
    Red, White, and Blue!

RECESSIONAL

RUDYARD KIPLING

God of our fathers, known of old,
    Lord of our far-flung battle-line,
Beneath whose awful Hand we hold
    Dominion over palm and pine—
Lord God of Hosts, be with us yet,
Lest we forget—lest we forget!

The tumult and the shouting dies;
    The Captains and the Kings depart:
Still stands Thine ancient sacrifice,
    An humble and a contrite heart.
Lord God of Hosts, be with us yet,
Lest we forget—lest we forget!

Far-called, our navies melt away;
    On dune and headland sinks the fire:
Lo, all our pomp of yesterday
    Is one with Nineveh and Tyre!
Judge of the Nations, spare us yet,
Lest we forget—lest we forget!

If, drunk with sight of power, we loose
  Wild tongues that have not Thee in awe,
Such boasting as the Gentiles use,
  Or lesser breeds without the Law—
Lord God of Hosts, be with us yet,
Lest we forget—lest we forget!

For heathen heart that puts her trust
  In reeking tube and iron shard,
All valiant dust that builds on dust,
  And guarding calls not Thee to guard,
For frantic boast and foolish word—
Thy mercy on Thy People, Lord!

TO AMERICA

On a Proposed Alliance between Two Great Nations

ALFRED AUSTIN

What is the voice I hear
  On the winds of the western sea?
Sentinel, listen from out Cape Clear
  And say what the voice may be.
  "'Tis a proud free people calling loud to a people proud
    and free.

"And it says to them: 'Kinsmen, hail!
  We severed have been too long.
Now let us have done with a worn-out tale—
  The tale of an ancient wrong—
  And our friendship last long as our love doth last, and be
    stronger than death is strong.'"

Answer them, sons of the self-same race,
    And blood of the self-same clan;
Let us speak with each other face to face
    And answer as man to man,
    And loyally love and trust each other as none but free
      men can.

Now fling them out to the breeze,
    Shamrock, Thistle, and Rose,
And the Star-Spangled Banner unfurl with these—
    A message to friends and foes
    Wherever the sails of peace are seen and wherever the war
      wind blows—

A message to bond and thrall to wake,
    For whenever we come, we twain,
The throne of the tyrant shall rock and quake,
    And his menace be void and vain,
    For you are lords of a strong young land, and we are lords
      of the main.

Yes, this is the voice of the bluff March gale:
    "We severed have been too long,
But now we have done with a worn-out tale—
    The tale of an ancient wrong—
    And our friendship shall last as love doth last, and be
      stronger than death is strong."

PRINCETON

ALFRED NOYES

Here Freedom stood by slaughtered friend and foe,
    And, ere the wrath paled or that sunset died,
Looked through the ages; then, with eyes aglow,
    Laid them to wait that future, side by side.[1]

Now lamp-lit gardens in the blue dusk shine
    Through dogwood, red and white;
And round the gray quadrangles, line by line,
    The windows fill with light,
Where Princeton calls to Magdalen, tower to tower,
    Twin lanthorns of the law;
And those cream-white magnolia boughs embower
    The halls of Old Nassau.

The dark bronze tigers crouch on either side
    Where redcoats used to pass;
And round the bird-loved house where Mercer died,
    And violets dusk the grass,
By Stony Brook that ran so red of old,
    But sings of friendship now,
To feed the old enemy's harvest fifty-fold
    The green earth takes the flow.

Through this May night, if one great ghost should stray
    With deep remembering eyes,
Where that old meadow of battle smiles away
    Its blood-stained memories,

[1] Lines for a monument to the American and British soldiers of the Revolutionary War who fell on the Princeton battlefield and were buried in one grave.

If Washington should walk where friend and foe
    Sleep and forget the past,
Be sure his unquenched heart would leap to know
    Their souls are linked at last.

Be sure, he walks, in shadowy buff and blue,
    Where these dim lilacs wave.
He bends his head to bless, as dreams come true,
    The promise of that grave;
Then, with a vaster hope than thought can scan,
    Touching his ancient sword,
Prays for that mightier realm of God in man:
    "Hasten Thy kingdom, Lord.

"Land of our hope, land of the singing stars,
    Type of the world to be,
The vision of a world set free from wars
    Takes life, takes form from thee;
Where all the jarring nations of this earth,
    Beneath the all-blessing sun,
Bring the new music of mankind to birth,
    And make the whole world one."

And those old comrades rise around him there,
    Old foemen, side by side,
With eyes like stars upon the brave night air,
    And young as when they died,
To hear your bells, O beautiful Princeton towers,
    Ring for the world's release.
They see you piercing like gray swords through flowers,
    And smile, from souls at peace.

HOME THOUGHTS FROM EUROPE

HENRY VAN DYKE

'Tis fine to see the Old World, and travel up and down
Among the famous palaces and cities of renown,
To admire the crumbly castles and the statues of the kings,—
But now I think I've had enough of antiquated things.

So it's home again, and home again, America for me!
My heart is turning home again, and there I long to be,
In the land of youth and freedom beyond the ocean bars,
Where the air is full of sunlight and the flag is full of stars.

Oh, London is a man's town, there's power in the air;
And Paris is a woman's town, with flowers in her hair;
And it's sweet to dream in Venice, and it's great to study
    Rome;
But when it comes to living, there is no place like Home.

I like the German fir-woods, in green battalions drilled;
I like the gardens of Versailles with flashing fountains filled;
But, oh, to take your hand, my dear, and ramble for a
    day
In the friendly western woodland where Nature has her
    way!

I know that Europe's wonderful, yet something seems to
    lack;
The Past is too much with her, and the people looking back,
But the glory of the Present is to make the Future free,—
We love our land for what she is and what she is to be.

Oh, it's home again, and home again, America for me!
I want a ship that's westward bound to plough the rolling sea
To the blessed land of Room Enough beyond the ocean bars,
Where the air is full of sunlight and the flag is full of stars.

A BALLAD OF HEROES

AUSTIN DOBSON

Because you passed, and now are not,—
  Because, in some remoter day,
Your sacred dust from doubtful spot
  Was blown of ancient airs away,—
  Because you perished,—must men say
Your deeds were naught, and so profane
  Your lives with that cold burden? Nay,
The deeds you wrought are not in vain!

Though, it may be, above the plot
  That hid your once imperial clay,
No greener than o'er men forgot
  The unregarding grasses sway;—
  Though there no sweeter is the lay
From careless bird,—though you remain
  Without distinction of decay,—
The deeds you wrought are not in vain!

No. For while yet in tower or cot
  Your story stirs the pulses' play;
And men forget the sordid lot—
  The sordid care, of cities gray;—

While yet, beset in homelier fray,
They learn from you the lesson plain
   That Life may go, so Honor stay,—
The deeds you wrought are not in vain!

ENVOY

Heroes of old! I humbly lay
   The laurel on your graves again;
Whatever men have done, men may,—
   The deeds you wrought are not in vain!

HEROES

LAURENCE HOUSMAN

Fair is their fame who stand in earth's high places,
   Rulers of men, strong-armed to break and bind.
Fairer the light that shines from comrade faces:
   Those we have loved, and lost, and kept in mind.

These be our heroes, hearts unnamed in story,
   Foot-firm that stood, and swerved not from the right;
Though in the world's eyes they attained no glory,
   Girt to their goal they gained the wished-for height.

Now for reward no after-age shall sunder
   These from their right to rest without a name.
Wide are the wings of heaven which fold them under,
   Who to the Winds of God resign their fame.

Blow, ye great Winds! Where'er man's spirit labors
   Breathe on his lips breath from the life they spent!
Comrades to all their kind, dear friends and neighbors,
   There, where the work goes well, they rest content.

They are the race,—they are the race immortal,
  Whose beams make broad the common light of day!
Though Time may dim, though Death hath barred their
    portal,
  These we salute, which nameless passed away.

COMRADES

RICHARD HOVEY

Comrades, pour the wine to-night
  For the parting is with dawn!
Oh, the clink of cups together,
  With the daylight coming on!
    Greet the morn
    With a double horn,
When strong men drink together!

Comrades, gird your swords to-night,
  For the battle is with dawn!
Oh, the clash of swords together,
  With the triumph coming on!
    Greet the foe,
    And lay him low,
When strong men fight together!

Comrades, watch the tides to-night,
  For the sailing is with dawn!
Oh, to face the spray together,
  With the tempest coming on!
    Greet the sea
    With a shout of glee,
When strong men roam together!

Comrades, give a cheer to-night,
　For the dying is with dawn!
Oh, to meet the stars together,
　With the silence coming on!
　　Greet the end
　　As a friend a friend,
When strong men die together!

THE SOLDIER

RUPERT BROOKE

If I should die, think only this of me:
　That there's some corner of a foreign field
That is for ever England.　There shall be
　In that rich earth a richer dust concealed;
A dust whom England bore, shaped, made aware,
　Gave, once, her flowers to love, her ways to roam,
A body of England's, breathing English air,
　Washed by the rivers, blest by suns of home.

And think, this heart, all evil shed away,
　A pulse in the eternal mind, no less
　　Gives somewhere back the thoughts by England given;
Her sights and sounds; dreams happy as her day;
　And laughter, learnt of friends; and gentleness,
　　In hearts at peace, under an English heaven.

IN FLANDERS FIELDS[1]

John McCrae

In Flanders fields the poppies blow
Between the crosses, row on row,
    That mark our place; and in the sky
    The larks, still bravely singing, fly
Scarce heard amid the guns below.

We are the Dead. Short days ago
We lived, felt dawn, saw sunset glow,
    Loved and were loved, and now we lie
        In Flanders fields.

Take up our quarrel with the foe:
To you from failing hands we throw
    The torch; be yours to hold it high.
    If ye break faith with us who die
We shall not sleep, though poppies grow
        In Flanders fields.

AMERICA'S REPLY

R. W. Lillard

Rest ye in peace, ye Flanders dead.
The fight that ye so bravely led
    We've taken up. And we will keep
    True faith with you who lie asleep
Each with a cross to mark his bed

[1] From "In Flanders Fields, and Other Poems," by John McCrae.
Courtesy of G. P. Putnam's Sons, Publishers, New York and London.

And poppies blowing overhead
Where once his own life-blood ran red.
So let your rest be sweet and deep
In Flanders fields.

Fear not that ye have died for naught.
The torch ye threw to us we caught.
Ten million hands will hold it high
And Freedom's light will never die;
We've learned the lesson that ye taught
In Flanders fields.

A FLANDERS GRAVE

Nathaniel Nathanson

To Lieutenant Colonel John McCrae, author of "In Flanders Fields."
Buried there in 1918.

In Flanders fields peace reigns to-night;
Quiet are they who led the fight—
And bravely fought, but had to die,
That Freedom's banner still should fly
And Justice triumph over Might.

Upon one grave by moon made bright,
God looks down from an unknown height,
Where now one sleeps who wished to lie
In Flanders fields.

Where poppies bloomed, there now is white—
For snow adds glory to the site
Of his grave who in days flown by
Had loved those fields where skylarks fly.
He sleeps now, in the calm moonlight
In Flanders fields.

RED POPPIES IN THE CORN

W. Campbell Galbraith

I've seen them in the morning light,
  When white mists drifted by:
I've seen them in the dusk o' night
  Glow 'gainst the starry sky.
The slender waving blossoms red,
  Mid yellow fields forlorn:
A glory on the scene they shed,
  Red Poppies in the Corn.

I've seen them, too, these blossoms red,
  Show 'gainst the trench lines' screen,
A crimson stream that waved and spread
  Through all the brown and green:
I've seen them dyed a deeper hue
  Than ever nature gave,
Shell-torn from slopes on which they grew,
  To cover many a grave.

Bright blossoms fair by nature set
  Along the dusty ways,
You cheered us, in the battle's fret,
  Through long and weary days:
You gave us hope: if fate be kind,
  We'll see that longed-for morn,
When home again we march and find
  Red Poppies in the Corn.

"I HAVE A RENDEZVOUS WITH DEATH"

Alan Seeger

I have a rendezvous with Death
At some disputed barricade,
When Spring comes round with rustling shade
And apple blossoms fill the air—
I have a rendezvous with Death
When Spring brings back blue days and fair.

It may be he shall take my hand
And lead me into his dark land
And close my eyes and quench my breath—
It may be I shall pass him still.
I have a rendezvous with Death
On some scarred slope of battered hill,
When Spring comes round again this year
And the first meadow-flowers appear.

God knows 'twere better to be deep
Pillowed in silk and scented down,
Where Love throbs out in blissful sleep,
Pulse nigh to pulse, and breath to breath,
Where hushed awakenings are dear. . . .
But I've a rendezvous with Death
At midnight in some flaming town,
When Spring trips north again this year,
And I to my pledged word am true,
I shall not fail that rendezvous.

VITAI LAMPADA[1]

HENRY NEWBOLT

There's a breathless hush in the Close to-night:
  Ten to make and the match to win—
A bumping pitch and a blinding light,
  An hour to play and the last man in.
And it's not for the sake of a ribboned coat,
  Or the selfish hope of a season's fame,
But his captain's hand on his shoulder smote:
  "Play up! play up! and play the game!"

The sand of the desert is sodden red,
  Red with the wreck of a square that broke;
The gatling's jammed and the colonel dead,
  And the regiment blind with dust and smoke.
The river of death has brimmed his banks,
  And England's far, and Honor a name,
But the voice of a schoolboy rallies the ranks:
  "Play up! play up! and play the game!"

This is the word that year by year,
  While in her place the school is set,
Every one of her sons must hear,
  And none that hears it dare forget.
This they all with a joyful mind
  Bear through life like a torch in flame,
And falling fling to the host behind:
  "Play up! play up! and play the game!"

[1] *Vitai Lampada*: "the torch of life." *Et quasi cursores vitai lampada tradunt*: "And like runners they hand on the torch of life" (LUCRETIUS, Bk. II, line 279). The image is taken from Plato's "Passing life on as if it were a torch."

THE SPIRES OF OXFORD

Winifred M. Letts

I saw the spires of Oxford
  As I was passing by,
The gray spires of Oxford
  Against the pearl-gray sky;
My heart was with the Oxford men
  Who went abroad to die.

The years go fast in Oxford,
  The golden years and gay,
The hoary Colleges look down
  On careless boys at play.
But when the bugles sounded—War!
  They put their games away.

They left the peaceful river,
  The cricket-field, the quad,
The shaven lawns of Oxford,
  To seek a bloody sod.
They gave their merry youth away
  For country and for God.

God rest you, happy gentlemen,
  Who laid your good lives down,
Who took the khaki and the gun
  Instead of cap and gown.
God bring you to a fairer place
  Than even Oxford town.

IN PRAISE OF THE ROYAL SCOTS FUSILIERS

JOHN BUCHAN

Ye'll a' hae heard tell o' the Fusilier Jocks,
 The famous auld Fusilier Jocks!
  They're as stieve as a stane,
  And as teuch as a bane,
 And as gleg as a pair o' muircocks.
They're maistly as braid as they're lang.
And the Gairman's a pump off the fang
 When he faces the fire in their ee.
  They're no verra bonny,
  I question if ony
Mair terrible sicht ye could see
Than a chairge o' the Fusilier Jocks.
  It gars Hindenburg swear
  "Gott in Himmel, nae mair
O' thae sudden and scan'alous shocks!"
  And the cannon o' Krupp
  Ane and a' they shut up
Like a pentit bit jaick-in-the-box,
At the rush o' the Fusilier Jocks.

The Kaiser he says to his son
 (The auld ane that looks like a fox)—
  "I went ower far
  When I stertit this war,
 Forgettin' the Fusilier Jocks.
I could manage the French and Italians and Poles,
The Russians and Tartars and yellow Mongols,
The Serbs and the Belgians, the English and Greeks,
And even the lads that gang wantin' the breeks;

But what o' thae Fusilier Jocks,
That stopna for duntin' and knocks?
        They'd rin wi' a yell
        Ower the plainstanes o' Hell;
They're no men ava—they are rocks!
        They'd gang barefit
        Through the Bottomless Pit,
And they'll tak Berlin in their socks,—
Will thae terrible Fusilier Jocks!" . . .

a': all; *stieve:* obstinate; *teuch:* tough; *gleg:* active; *braid:* broad; *off the fang:* out of gear; *ony:* any; *gars:* causes; *pentit bit jaick-in-the box:* painted little jack-in-the-box; *stertit:* started; *gang wantin' the breeks:* go without trousers; *thae:* those; *stopna:* stop not; *duntin':* thumping; *ava:* at all; *barefit:* barefoot.

VIVE LA FRANCE!

CHARLOTTE HOLMES CRAWFORD

Franceline rose in the dawning gray,
And her heart would dance though she knelt to pray,
For her man Michel had holiday,
        Fighting for France.

She offered her prayer by the cradle-side,
And with baby palms folded in hers she cried:
"If I have but one prayer, dear, crucified
        Christ—save France!

"But if I have two, then, by Mary's grace,
Carry me safe to the meeting place,
Let me look once again on my dear love's face,
        Save him for France!"

She crooned to her boy: "Oh, how glad he'll be,
Little three-months-old, to set eyes on thee!
For, 'Rather than gold, would I give,' wrote he,
    'A son to France.'

"Come, now, be good, little stray *sauterelle*,
For we're going by-by to thy papa Michel,
But I'll not say where, for fear thou wilt tell,
    Little pigeon of France!

"Six days' leave and a year between!
But what would you have? In six days clean,
Heaven was made," said Franceline,
    "Heaven and France."

She came to the town of the nameless name,
To the marching troops in the streets she came,
And she held high her boy like a taper flame
    Burning for France.

Fresh from the trenches and gray with grime,
Silent they march like a pantomime;
"But what need of music? My heart beats time—
    Vive la France!"

His regiment comes. Oh, then where is he?
"There is dust in my eyes, for I cannot see,—
Is that my Michel to the right of thee,
    Soldier of France?"

Then out of the ranks a comrade fell,—
"Yesterday—'twas a splinter of shell—
And he whispered thy name, did thy poor Michel,
    Dying for France."

The tread of the troops on the pavement throbbed
Like a woman's heart of its last joy robbed,
As she lifted her boy to the flag, and sobbed:
　　"Vive—la—France!"

PRAYER DURING BATTLE

HERMANN HAGEDORN

Lord, in this hour of tumult,
　　Lord, in this night of fears,
Keep open, oh, keep open
　　My eyes, my ears.

Not blindly, not in hatred,
　　Lord, let me do my part.
Keep open, oh, keep open
　　My mind, my heart!

THE HEART-CRY

FRANCIS W. BOURDILLON

She turned the page of wounds and death
With trembling fingers. In a breath
The gladness of her life became
Naught but a memory and a name.

Farewell! Farewell! I might not share
The perils it was yours to dare.
Dauntless you fronted death; for me
Rests to face life as fearlessly.

KILMENY

A Song of the Trawlers

ALFRED NOYES

Dark, dark lay the drifters against the red West,
  As they shot their long meshes of steel overside;
And the oily green waters were rocking to rest
  When *Kilmeny* went out, at the turn of the tide.
And nobody knew where that lassie would roam,
  For the magic that called her was tapping unseen.
It was well-nigh a week ere *Kilmeny* came home,
  And nobody knew where *Kilmeny* had been.

She'd a gun at her bow that was Newcastle's best,
  And a gun at her stern that was fresh from the Clyde,
And a secret a skipper had never confessed,
  Not even at dawn, to his newly-wed bride;
And a wireless that whispered above like a gnome,
  The laughter of London, the boasts of Berlin.
O, it may have been mermaids that lured her from home,
  But nobody knew where *Kilmeny* had been.

It was dark when *Kilmeny* came home from her quest,
  With her bridge dabbled red where her skipper had died;
But she moved like a bride with a rose at the breast;
  And "Well done, *Kilmeny*!" the admiral cried.
Now at sixty-four fathom a conger may come,
  And nose at the bones of a drowned submarine;
But late in the evening *Kilmeny* came home,
  And nobody knew where *Kilmeny* had been.

There's a wandering shadow that stares at the foam,
　　Though they sing all the night to old England, their queen,
Late, late in the evening *Kilmeny* came home,
　　And nobody knew where *Kilmeny* had been.

THE LAST PILOT

DUNCAN TOVEY

Overhead, in a tranquil sky, out of the sunset glow,
The stately battle-planes go sailing east, against the foe,
And the quivering air is all a-drone, like an organ, deep and
　　low.

The sunset gleams on the old bell-tower and the roofs of the
　　old French town :
Gleams and fades, and the shadows fall, as the night comes
　　creeping down,
And the German line in the twilight glooms distant and dark
　　and brown.

One by one, their duty done, the planes come back from the
　　fight ;
One by one, like homing birds, back through the darkening
　　night,
And twinkling against the fading West, goes up their guiding
　　light.

Hour by hour the light goes up, flashing the signal far,
But the Last Pilot heeds it not. His ship has crossed the bar,
And he has found eternal peace in the light of his Heavenly
　　Star.

THE DEAD TO THE LIVING

Laurence Binyon

O you that still have rain and sun,
Kisses of children and of wife,
And the good earth to tread upon,
And the mere sweetness that is life,
Forget not us, who gave all these
For something dearer, and for you.
Think in what cause we crossed the seas!
Remember, he who fails the Challenge
Fails us, too.

Now in the hour that shows the strong—
The soul no evil powers affray—
Drive straight against embattled wrong!
Faith knows but one, the hardest, way.
Endure; the end is worth the throe,
Give, give, and dare; and again dare!
On, to that Wrong's great overthrow.
We are with you, of you; we the pain
And victory share.

THE SUPREME SACRIFICE

John Stanhope Arkwright

O valiant Hearts, who to your glory came
Through dust of conflict and through battle-flame;
Tranquil you lie, your knightly virtue proved,
Your memory hallowed in the Land you loved.

Proudly you gathered, rank on rank to war,
As who had heard God's message from afar;
All you had hoped for, all you had, you gave
To save Mankind—yourselves you scorned to save.

Splendid you passed, the great surrender made,
Into the light that nevermore shall fade;
Deep your contentment in that blest abode,
Who wait the last clear trumpet-call of God.

Long years ago, as earth lay dark and still,
Rose a loud cry upon a lonely hill,
While in the frailty of our human clay
Christ, our Redeemer, passed the self-same way.

Still stands His Cross from that dread hour to this
Like some bright star above the dark abyss;
Still, through the veil, the Victor's pitying eyes ·
Look down to bless our Lesser Calvaries.

These were His servants, in His steps they trod
Following through death the martyr'd Son of God:
Victor He rose; victorious too shall rise
They who have drunk His cup of Sacrifice.

O risen Lord, O Shepherd of our Dead,
Whose Cross has brought them and whose Staff has
        led—
In glorious hope their proud and sorrowing Land
Commits her Children to Thy gracious hand.

REVEILLÉ

EDEN PHILLPOTTS

Ended the watches of the night; oh, hear the bugles blow —
  The bugles blow Reveillé at the golden gates of morn;
A shudder moves the living East; the stars are burning low
  Above the crystal cradle of a day that's newly born.
Arise, ye slumbering legions; wake for honor and for right;
  Awake, arise, ye myriad men, to faith and justice sworn;
High heaven's fires are flashing on the valley and the height,
  And the bugles blow Reveillé at the golden gates of morn.

Within the holy of your hearts, oh, hear the bugles blow—
  The bugles blow Reveillé at the golden gates of morn,
And welcome with their clarion ineffable foreglow
  Of a sunrise where the souls of men are being newly born.
Awake, arise, ye legions, to the challenge of the dead;
  Arise, awake, and follow in the footsteps they have worn;
For their spirits are the glory of the dayspring overhead,
  And their bugles blow Reveillé at the golden gates of morn.

BALLADS AND NARRATIVE POEMS

"THE HIGHWAYMAN CAME RIDING—RIDING—RIDING—"

(PAGE 38)

THE BALLAD OF EAST AND WEST

Rudyard Kipling

*Oh, East is East, and West is West, and never the twain shall
    meet,*
*Till Earth and Sky stand presently at God's great Judgment
    Seat;*
*But there is neither East nor West, Border, nor Breed, nor
    Birth,*
*When two strong men stand face to face, though they come
    from the ends of the earth!*

Kamal is out with twenty men to raise the Border side,
And he has lifted the Colonel's mare that is the Colonel's
    pride;
He has lifted her out of the stable-door between the dawn
    and the day,
And turned the calkins upon her feet, and ridden her far
    away.
Then up and spoke the Colonel's son that led a troop of the
    Guides:
"Is there never a man of all my men can say where Kamal
    hides?"
Then up and spoke Mohammed Khan, the son of the Res-
    saldar:
"If ye know the track of the morning mist, ye know where his
    pickets are.

At dusk he harries the Abazai—at dawn he is into Bonair,
But he must go by Fort Bukloh to his own place to fare,
So if ye gallop to Fort Bukloh as fast as a bird can fly,
By the favor of God ye may cut him off ere he win to the
    Tongue of Jagai.
But if he be past the Tongue of Jagai, right swiftly turn ye
    then,
For the length and the breadth of that grisly plain is sown
    with Kamal's men.
There is rock to the left, and rock to the right, and low lean
    thorn between,
And ye may hear a breech-bolt snick where never a man is
    seen."
The Colonel's son has taken a horse, and a raw rough dun
    was he,
With the mouth of a bell and the heart of Hell and the head
    of a gallows-tree.
The Colonel's son to the Fort has won, they bid him stay to
    eat—
Who rides at the tail of a Border thief, he sits not long at his
    meat.
He's up and away from Fort Bukloh as fast as he can fly,
Till he was aware of his father's mare in the gut of the Tongue
    of Jagai,
Till he was aware of his father's mare with Kamal upon her
    back,
And when he could spy the white of her eye, he made the
    pistol crack.
He has fired once, he has fired twice, but the whistling ball
    went wide.
"Ye shoot like a soldier," Kamal said. "Show now if ye can
    ride."
It's up and over the Tongue of Jagai, as blown dust-devils go.

The dun he fled like a stag of ten, but the mare like a barren
  doe,
The dun he leaned against the bit and slugged his head above,
But the red mare played with the snaffle-bars, as a maiden
  plays with a glove.
There was rock to the left and rock to the right, and low lean
  thorn between,
And thrice he heard a breech-bolt snick though never a man
  was seen.
They have ridden the low moon out of the sky, their hoofs
  drum up the dawn,
The dun he went like a wounded bull, but the mare like a
  new-roused fawn.
The dun he fell at a water-course—in a woeful heap fell he,
And Kamal has turned the red mare back, and pulled the
  rider free.
He has knocked the pistol out of his hand—small room was
  there to strive,
"'Twas only by favor of mine," quoth he, "ye rode so long
  alive:
There was not a rock for twenty mile, there was not a clump
  of tree,
But covered a man of my own men with his rifle cocked on
  his knee.
If I had raised my bridle-hand, as I have held it low,
The little jackals that flee so fast were feasting all in a row:
If I had bowed my head on my breast, as I have held it high,
The kite that whistles above us now were gorged till she
  could not fly."
Lightly answered the Colonel's son: "Do good to bird and
  beast,
But count who come for the broken meats before thou makest
  a feast.

If there should follow a thousand swords to carry my bones
    away,
Belike the price of a jackal's meal were more than a thief
    could pay.
They will feed their horse on the standing crop, their men on
    the garnered grain.
The thatch of the byres will serve their fires when all the
    cattle are slain.
But if thou thinkest the price be fair,—thy brethren wait to
    sup,
The hound is kin to the jackal-spawn,—howl, dog, and call
    them up!
And if thou thinkest the price be high, in steer and gear and
    stack,
Give me my father's mare again, and I'll fight my own way
    back!"
Kamal has gripped him by the hand and set him upon his feet.
"No talk shall be of dogs," said he, "when wolf and gray wolf
    meet.
May I eat dirt if thou hast hurt of me in deed or breath;
What dam of lances brought thee forth to jest at the dawn
    with Death?"
Lightly answered the Colonel's son: "I hold by the blood of
    my clan:
Take up the mare for my father's gift—by God, she has
    carried a man!"
The red mare ran to the Colonel's son, and nuzzled against
    his breast;
"We be two strong men," said Kamal then, "but she loveth
    the younger best.
So she shall go with a lifter's dower, my turquoise-studded rein,
My broidered saddle and saddle-cloth, and silver stirrups
    twain."

The Colonel's son a pistol drew, and held it muzzle-end,

"Ye have taken the one from a foe," said he; "will ye take
the mate from a friend?"

"A gift for a gift," said Kamal straight; "a limb for the risk
of a limb.

Thy father has sent his son to me, I'll send my son to him!"

With that he whistled his only son, that dropped from a
mountain-crest—

He trod the ling like a buck in spring, and he looked like a
lance in rest.

"Now here is thy master," Kamal said, "who leads a troop
of the Guides,

And thou must ride at his left side as shield on shoulder
rides.

Till Death or I cut loose the tie, at camp and board and bed,

Thy life is his—thy fate it is to guard him with thy head.

So thou must eat the White Queen's meat, and all her foes
are thine,

And thou must harry thy father's hold for the peace of the
Border-line,

And thou must make a trooper tough and hack thy way to
power—

Belike they will raise thee to Ressaldar when I am hanged
in Peshawur."

They have looked each other between the eyes, and there
they found no fault,

They have taken the Oath of the Brother-in-Blood on leav-
ened bread and salt:

They have taken the Oath of the Brother-in-Blood on fire
and fresh-cut sod,

On the hilt and the haft of the Khyber knife, and the Wondrous Names of God.

The Colonel's son he rides the mare and Kamal's boy the dun,
And two have come back to Fort Bukloh where there went
   forth but one.
And when they drew to the Quarter-Guard, full twenty
   swords flew clear—
There was not a man but carried his feud with the blood of
   the mountaineer.
"Ha' done! ha' done!" said the Colonel's son. "Put up the
   steel at your sides!
Last night ye had struck at a Border thief—to-night 'tis a
   man of the Guides!"

*Oh, East is East, and West is West, and never the twain shall
   meet,*
*Till Earth and Sky stand presently at God's great Judgment
   Seat;*
*But there is neither East nor West, Border, nor Breed, nor
   Birth,*
*When two strong men stand face to face, though they come
   from the ends of the earth!*

THE HIGHWAYMAN

ALFRED NOYES

PART I

The wind was a torrent of darkness among the gusty trees,
The moon was a ghostly galleon tossed upon cloudy seas,
The road was a ribbon of moonlight over the purple moor,
And the highwayman came riding—
      Riding—riding—
The highwayman came riding, up to the old inn-door.

He'd a French cocked-hat on his forehead, a bunch of lace
    at his chin,
A coat of the claret velvet, and breeches of brown doe-skin;
They fitted with never a wrinkle: his boots were up to the
    thigh!
And he rode with a jeweled twinkle,
        His pistol butts a-twinkle,
His rapier hilt a-twinkle, under the jeweled sky.

Over the cobbles he clattered and clashed in the dark inn-yard,
And he tapped with his whip on the shutters, but all was
    locked and barred;
He whistled a tune to the window, and who should be waiting
    there
But the landlord's black-eyed daughter,
        Bess, the landlord's daughter,
Plaiting a dark red love-knot into her long black hair.

And dark in the dark old inn-yard a stable-wicket creaked
Where Tim the ostler listened; his face was white and peaked;
His eyes were hollows of madness, his hair like mouldy hay,
But he loved the landlord's daughter,
        The landlord's red-lipped daughter,
Dumb as a dog he listened, and he heard the robber say—

"One kiss, my bonny sweetheart, I'm after a prize to-night,
But I shall be back with the yellow gold before the morning
    light;
Yet, if they press me sharply, and harry me through the day,
Then look for me by moonlight,
        Watch for me by moonlight,
I'll come to thee by moonlight, though hell should bar the
    way."

He rose upright in the stirrups; he scarce could reach her
hand,
But she loosened her hair i' the casement! His face burnt
like a brand
As the black cascade of perfume came tumbling over his
breast;
And he kissed its waves in the moonlight,
(Oh, sweet black waves in the moonlight!)
Then he tugged at his rein in the moonlight, and galloped
away to the west.

PART II

He did not come in the dawning; he did not come at noon;
And out o' the tawny sunset, before the rise o' the moon,
When the road was a gipsy's ribbon, looping the purple moor,
A red-coat troop came marching—
Marching—marching—
King George's men came marching, up to the old inn-door.

They said no word to the landlord, they drank his ale instead,
But they gagged his daughter and bound her to the foot of
her narrow bed;
Two of them knelt at her casement, with muskets at their
side!
There was death at every window;
And hell at one dark window;
For Bess could see, through her casement, the road that *he*
would ride.

They had tied her up to attention, with many a sniggering
jest;
They had bound a musket beside her, with the barrel beneath
her breast!

"Now keep good watch!" and they kissed her. She heard
    the dead man say—
Look for me by moonlight;
        Watch for me by moonlight;
I'll come to thee by moonlight, though hell should bar the
    way!

She twisted her hands behind her; but all the knots held
    good!
She writhed her hands till her fingers were wet with sweat or
    blood!
They stretched and strained in the darkness, and the hours
    crawled by like years,
Till, now, on the stroke of midnight,
        Cold, on the stroke of midnight,
The tip of one finger touched it! The trigger at least was
    hers!

The tip of one finger touched it; she strove no more for the
    rest!
Up, she stood up to attention, with the barrel beneath her
    breast,
She would not risk their hearing; she would not strive again;
For the road lay bare in the moonlight;
        Blank and bare in the moonlight;
And the blood of her veins in the moonlight throbbed to her
    love's refrain.

Tlot-tlot; tlot-tlot! Had they heard it? The horse-hoofs
    ringing clear;
Tlot-tlot, tlot-tlot, in the distance? Were they deaf that
    they did not hear?

Down the ribbon of moonlight, over the brow of the hill,
The highwayman came riding,
             Riding, riding!
The red-coats looked to their priming! She stood up, straight
    and still!

Tlot-tlot, in the frosty silence! *Tlot-tlot*, in the echoing
    night!
Nearer he came and nearer! Her face was like a light!
Her eyes grew wide for a moment; she drew one last deep
    breath,
Then her finger moved in the moonlight,
             Her musket shattered the moonlight,
Shattered her breast in the moonlight and warned him—with
    her death.

He turned; he spurred to the west; he did not know who
    stood
Bowed, with her head o'er the musket, drenched with her own
    red blood!
Not till the dawn he heard it, his face grew grey to hear
How Bess, the landlord's daughter,
             The landlord's black-eyed daughter,
Had watched for her love in the moonlight, and died in the
    darkness there.

Back, he spurred like a madman, shrieking a curse to the
    sky,
With the white road smoking behind him, and his rapier
    brandished high!
Blood-red were his spurs i' the golden noon; wine-red was his
    velvet coat,

When they shot him down on the highway,
> Down like a dog on the highway,
And he lay in his blood on the highway, with the bunch of
lace at his throat.

. . . .

And still of a winter's night, they say, when the wind is in the
trees,
When the moon is a ghostly galleon tossed upon cloudy seas,
When the road is a ribbon of moonlight over the purple moor,
A highwayman comes riding—
> *Riding—riding—*
A highwayman comes riding, up to the old inn-door.

Over the cobbles he clatters and clangs in the dark inn-yard;
And he taps with his whip on the shutters, but all is locked
and barred;
He whistles a tune to the window, and who should be waiting
there
But the landlord's black-eyed daughter,
> *Bess, the landlord's daughter,*
Plaiting a dark red love-knot into her long black hair.

LEPANTO[1]

GILBERT KEITH CHESTERTON

White founts falling in the Courts of the sun,
And the Soldan of Byzantium is smiling as they run;
There is laughter like the fountains in that face of all men
feared,
It stirs the forest darkness, the darkness of his beard;
It curls the blood-red crescent, the crescent of his lips;

[1] By arrangement with Messrs. Burns, Oates and Washbourne, London.

For the inmost sea of all the earth is shaken with his ships.
They have dared the white republics up the capes of Italy,
They have dashed the Adriatic round the Lion of the Sea,
And the Pope has cast his arms abroad for agony and loss,
And called the kings of Christendom for swords about the Cross.
The cold queen of England is looking in the glass;
The shadow of the Valois is yawning at the Mass;
From evening isles fantastical rings faint the Spanish gun,
And the Lord upon the Golden Horn is laughing in the sun.

Dim drums throbbing, in the hills half heard,
Where only on a nameless throne a crownless prince has stirred.
Where, risen from a doubtful seat and half attainted stall,
The last knight of Europe takes weapons from the wall,
The last and lingering troubadour to whom the bird has sung,
That once went singing southward when all the world was
    young.
In that enormous silence, tiny and unafraid,
Comes up along a winding road the noise of the Crusade.
Strong gongs groaning as the guns boom far,
Don John of Austria is going to the war,
Stiff flags straining in the night-blasts cold
In the gloom black-purple, in the glint old-gold,
Torchlight crimson on the copper kettle-drums,
Then the tuckets, then the trumpets, then the cannon, and
    he comes.
Don John laughing in the brave beard curled,
Spurning of his stirrups like the thrones of all the world,
Holding his head up for a flag of all the free.
Love-light of Spain—hurrah!
Death-light of Africa!
Don John of Austria
Is riding to the sea.

Mahound is in his paradise above the evening star,
(*Don John of Austria is going to the war.*)
He moves a mighty turban on the timeless houri's knees,
His turban that is woven of the sunsets and the seas.
He shakes the peacock gardens as he rises from his ease,
And he strides among the tree-tops and is taller than the
    trees;
And his voice through all the garden is a thunder sent to
    bring
Black Azrael and Ariel and Ammon on the wing.
Giants and the Genii,
Multiplex of wing and eye,
Whose strong obedience broke the sky
When Solomon was king.

They rush in red and purple from the red clouds of the morn,
From the temples where the yellow gods shut up their eyes in
    scorn;
They rise in green robes roaring from the green hells of the
    sea
Where fallen skies and evil hues and eyeless creatures be,
On them the sea-valves cluster and the grey sea-forests curl,
Splashed with a splendid sickness, the sickness of the pearl;
They swell in sapphire smoke out of the blue cracks of the
    ground,—
They gather and they wonder, and give worship to Mahound.
And he saith, "Break up the mountains where the hermit-
    folk can hide,
And sift the red and silver sands lest bone of saint abide,
And chase the Giaours flying night and day, not giving rest,
For that which was our trouble comes again out of the west.
We have set the seal of Solomon on all things under sun,
Of knowledge and of sorrow and endurance of things done.

But a noise is in the mountains, in the mountains, and I know
The voice that shook our palaces—four hundred years ago:
It is he that saith not 'Kismet'; it is he that knows not Fate;
It is Richard, it is Raymond, it is Godfrey at the gate!
It is he whose loss is laughter when he counts the wager
    worth,
Put down your feet upon him, that our peace be on the earth."
For he heard drums groaning and he heard guns jar,
(*Don John of Austria is going to the war.*)
Sudden and still—hurrah!
Bolt from Iberia!
Don John of Austria
Is gone by Alcalar.

St. Michael's on his Mountain in the sea-roads of the north
(*Don John of Austria is girt and going forth.*)
Where the grey seas glitter and the sharp tides shift
And the sea-folk labor and the red sails lift.
He shakes his lance of iron and he claps his wings of stone;
The noise is gone through Normandy; the noise is gone
    alone;
The North is full of tangled things and texts and aching eyes,
And dead is all the innocence of anger and surprise,
And Christian killeth Christian in a narrow dusty room,
And Christian dreadeth Christ that hath a newer face of doom,
And Christian hateth Mary that God kissed in Galilee,—
But Don John of Austria is riding to the sea.
Don John calling through the blast and the eclipse
Crying with the trumpet, with the trumpet of his lips,
Trumpet that sayeth *ha!*
      Domino gloria!
Don John of Austria
Is shouting to the ships.

King Philip's in his closet with the Fleece about his neck
(*Don John of Austria is armed upon the deck.*)
The walls are hung with velvet that is black and soft as sin,
And little dwarfs creep out of it and little dwarfs creep in.
He holds a crystal phial that has colors like the moon,
He touches, and it tingles, and he trembles very soon,
And his face is as a fungus of a leprous white and grey
Like plants in the high houses that are shuttered from the day,
And death is in the phial and the end of noble work,
But Don John of Austria has fired upon the Turk.
Don John's hunting, and his hounds have bayed—
Booms away past Italy the rumor of his raid.
Gun upon gun, ha! ha!
Gun upon gun, hurrah!
Don John of Austria
Has loosed the cannonade.

The Pope was in his chapel before day or battle broke,
(*Don John of Austria is hidden in the smoke.*)
The hidden room in man's house where God sits all the year,
The secret window whence the world looks small and very
   dear.
He sees as in a mirror on the monstrous twilight sea
The crescent of his cruel ships whose name is mystery;
They fling great shadows foe-wards, making Cross and Castle
   dark,
They veil the plumèd lions on the galleys of St. Mark;
And above the ships are palaces of brown, black-bearded
   chiefs,
And below the ships are prisons, where with multitudinous
   griefs,
Christian captives sick and sunless, all a laboring race repines
Like a race in sunken cities, like a nation in the mines.

They are lost like slaves that swat, and in the skies of
    morning hung
The stair-ways of the tallest gods when tyranny was young.
They are countless, voiceless, hopeless as those fallen or
    fleeing on
Before the high King's horses in the granite of Babylon.
And many a one grows witless in his quiet room in hell
Where a yellow face looks inward through the lattice of his
    cell,
And he finds his God forgotten, and he seeks no more a
    sign—
(*But Don John of Austria has burst the battle-line!*)
Don John pounding from the slaughter-painted poop,
Purpling all the ocean like a bloody pirate's sloop,
Scarlet running over on the silvers and the golds,
Breaking of the hatches up and bursting of the holds,
Thronging of the thousands up that labor under sea
White for bliss and blind for sun and stunned for liberty.
Vivat Hispania!
Domino Gloria!
Don John of Austria
Has set his people free!

Cervantes on his galley sets the sword back in the sheath
(*Don John of Austria rides homeward with a wreath.*)
And he sees across a weary land a straggling road in Spain,
Up which a lean and foolish knight for ever rides in vain,
And he smiles, but not as Sultans smile, and settles back the
    blade. . . .
(*But Don John of Austria rides home from the Crusade.*)

PATTERNS

AMY LOWELL

I walk down the garden paths,
And all the daffodils
Are blowing, and the bright blue squills.
I walk down the patterned garden paths
In my stiff, brocaded gown.
With my powdered hair and jeweled fan,
I too am a rare
Pattern. As I wander down
The garden paths.

My dress is richly figured,
And the train
Makes a pink and silver stain
On the gravel, and the thrift
Of the borders.
Just a plate of current fashion,
Tripping by in high-heeled, ribboned shoes.
Not a softness anywhere about me,
Only whalebone and brocade.
And I sink on a seat in the shade
Of a lime tree. For my passion
Wars against the stiff brocade.
The daffodils and squills
Flutter in the breeze
As they please.
And I weep;
For the lime tree is in blossom
And one small flower has dropped upon my bosom.

And the plashing of waterdrops
In the marble fountain
Comes down the garden paths.
The dropping never stops.
Underneath my stiffened gown
Is the softness of a woman bathing in a marble basin,
A basin in the midst of hedges grown
So thick she cannot see her lover hiding,
But she guesses he is near,
And the sliding of the water
Seems the stroking of a dear
Hand upon her.
What is Summer in a fine brocaded gown!
I should like to see it lying in a heap upon the ground.
All the pink and silver crumpled up on the ground.

I would be the pink and silver as I ran along the paths,
And he would stumble after,
Bewildered by my laughter.
I should see the sun flashing from his sword hilt and the
        buckles on his shoes.
I would choose
To lead him in a maze along the patterned paths,
A bright and laughing maze for my heavy-booted lover,
Till he caught me in the shade,
And the buttons of his waistcoat bruised my body as he
        clasped me,
Aching, melting, unafraid.
With the shadows of the leaves and the sundrops,
And the plopping of the waterdrops,
All about us in the open afternoon—

I am very like to swoon
With the weight of this brocade,
For the sun sifts through the shade.

Underneath the fallen blossom
In my bosom,
Is a letter I have hid.
It was brought to me this morning by a rider from the Duke.
"Madam, we regret to inform you that Lord Hartwell
Died in action Thursday se'nnight."
As I read it in the white morning sunlight,
The letters squirmed like snakes.
"Any answer, Madam?" said my footman.
"No," I told him.
"See that the messenger takes some refreshment.
No, no answer."

And I walked into the garden,
Up and down the patterned paths,
In my stiff, correct brocade.
The blue and yellow flowers stood up proudly in the sun,
Each one.
I stood upright too,
Held rigid to the pattern
By the stiffness of my gown.
Up and down I walked,
Up and down.

In a month he would have been my husband.
In a month, here, underneath this lime,
We would have broke the pattern;
He for me, and I for him,

He as Colonel, I as Lady,
On this shady seat.
He had a whim
That sunlight carried blessing.
And I answered, "It shall be as you have said."
Now he is dead.

In Summer and in Winter I shall walk
Up and down
The patterned garden paths
In my stiff, brocaded gown.
The squills and daffodils
Will give place to pillared roses, and to asters, and to snow.
I shall go
Up and down
In my gown.
Gorgeously arrayed,
Boned and stayed.
And the softness of my body will be guarded from embrace
By each button, hook, and lace.
For the man who should loose me is dead,
Fighting with the Duke of Flanders
In a pattern called a war.
Christ! What are patterns for?

HOME AND EARLY LIFE

"AN OLD LANE, AN OLD GATE, AN OLD HOUSE BY A TREE"
(PAGE 55)

THE OLD HOME

Madison Cawein

An old lane, an old gate, an old house by a tree;
A wild wood, a wild brook—they will not let me be:
In boyhood I knew them, and still they call to me.

Down deep in my heart's core I hear them, and my eyes
Through tear-mists behold them beneath the old-time skies,
'Mid bee-boom and rose-bloom and orchard-lands arise.

I hear them; and heartsick with longing is my soul,
To walk there, to dream there, beneath the sky's blue bowl;
Around me, within me, the weary world made whole.

To talk with the wild brook of all the long-ago;
To whisper the wood-wind of things we used to know
When we were old companions, before my heart knew woe.

To walk with the morning and watch its rose unfold;
To drowse with the noontide lulled in its heart of gold;
To lie with the night-time and dream the dreams of old.

To tell to the old trees, and to each listening leaf,
The longing, the yearning, as in my boyhood brief,
The old hope, the old love, would ease me of my grief.

The old lane, the old gate, the old house by the tree;
The wild wood, the wild brook—they will not let me be:
In boyhood I knew them, and still they call to me.

UPON THE HEARTH

Lloyd Mifflin

A tree will prove a blessing all life long;
    From birth to death it brings us naught but good;
    The shade will make a pleasant solitude
For one who lies and dreams the grass among;
What golden globes upon the limbs are hung
    In summer! and when dead, the burning wood
    Will foster sweetness in the poet's mood,
Hum on his hearth, and help his sylvan song.
Its death is like the day's, for still it throws
    A lingering light roseate around our rooms,
    As slow the fire its last of life consumes;
Then sinks to embers like the sunset snows,
And lying, even in its ashes, glows
    With bright remembrance of the spring-time blooms.

THE SACRAMENT OF FIRE[1]

John Oxenham

Kneel always when you light a fire!
Kneel reverently, and thankful be
For God's unfailing charity,
And on the ascending flame inspire
A little prayer, that shall upbear
The incense of your thankfulness
For this sweet grace

[1] From "The Fiery Cross," by John Oxenham. Copyright, 1918, by George H. Doran Company, Publishers.

Of warmth and light!
For here again is sacrifice
For your delight.

Within the wood,
That lived a joyous life
Through sunny days and rainy days
And winter storms and strife; —
Within the peat,
That drank the moorland sweet
Of bracken, whin, and sweet bell-heather,
And all the joy of gold gorse feather
Flaming like Love in wintriest weather,—
While snug below, in sun and snow,
Peat heard the beat of the padding feet
Of foal and dam, and ewe and lamb,
And the stamp of old bell-wether; —
Within the coal,
Where forests lie entombed,
Oak, elm, and chestnut, beech and red pine bole,—
God shrined His sunshine, and enwombed
For you these stores of light and heat,
Your life-joys to complete.
These all have died that you might live;
Yours now the high prerogative
To loose their long captivities,—
To give them new sweet span of life
And fresh activities.

Kneel always when you light a fire!
Kneel reverently,
And grateful be
To God for His unfailing charity!

A BIRTHNIGHT CANDLE

JOHN FINLEY

A candle, waiter! Thank you. No, 'tis not
To light a cigarette. I wish its flame
For better use. A little nearer, please,
For if the guests should see, they'd wonder—well,
But do you know that I have touched no wine
This hallowed night, the night the lad was born,—
Which ushers in each year great Lincoln's day.

The brilliant banquet-hall of myriad lamps
Will not deny me this one little blaze
From all its dazzling wealth to celebrate
His natal festival.

         Do you, perchance,
Not have this custom, *garçon*, in old France,
Of lighting candles on a birthday cake,
And quenching then each flame with some fond wish?
Well, I have said that wheresoe'er this night
O'ertook me exiled from his happy face,
I'd blow a candle out with such desire
As could have speech but in a lambent flame
Piercing the mystery of space about.—
The night has found me guest at this high feast,
Companioned of famed men, but with my thought
Ever of him and her who gave him birth.

And here's the candle!—For some holy rite
'Twas doubtless fashioned, and by hands that moved
In rhythm with some sweet song, molding the wax
Distilled by bees that roamed through flowered fields
In drowsy summer afternoons, to store

The precious fires from out the skies, and then
To give them perfume of the fragrant earth.

There! It has gone, and never light since God
Divided day from dark has borne a prayer
More ardent than this wish for him whose name
I, bearing, vow anew to keep from stain.

   .   .   .   .

Put back that candle in its golden cup.
No, thank you, waiter. No *liqueur* for me . . .
But just a little coffee. Yes, two lumps.
(The smoke is getting in my eyes.)
                     That's all.

SONGS FOR MY MOTHER

ANNA HEMPSTEAD BRANCH

I. HER HANDS

My mother's hands are cool and fair,
   They can do anything.
Delicate mercies hid them there
   Like flowers in the spring.

When I was small and could not sleep,
   She used to come to me,
And with my cheek upon her hand
   How sure my rest would be.

For everything she ever touched
   Of beautiful or fine,
Their memories living in her hands
   Would warm that sleep of mine.

Her hands remember how they played
    One time in meadow streams,—
And all the flickering song and shade
    Of water took my dreams.

Swift through her haunted fingers pass
    Memories of garden things;—
I dipped my face in flowers and grass
    And sounds of hidden wings.

One time she touched the cloud that kissed
    Brown pastures bleak and far;—
I leaned my cheek into a mist
    And thought I was a star.

All this was very long ago
    And I am grown; but yet
The hand that lured my slumber so
    I never can forget.

For still when drowsiness comes on,
    It seems so soft and cool,
Shaped happily beneath my cheek,
    Hollow and beautiful.

II. HER WORDS

My mother has the prettiest tricks
    Of words and words and words.
Her talk comes out as smooth and sleek
    As breasts of singing birds.

She shapes her speech all silver fine
    Because she loves it so.
And her own eyes begin to shine
    To hear her stories grow.

And if she goes to make a call
    Or out to take a walk,
We leave our work when she returns
    And run to hear her talk.

We had not dreamed these things were so
    Of sorrow and of mirth.
Her speech is as a thousand eyes
    Through which we see the earth.

God wove a web of loveliness,
    Of clouds and stars and birds,
But made not anything at all
    So beautiful as words.

They shine around our simple earth
    With golden shadowings,
And every common thing they touch
    Is exquisite with wings.

There's nothing poor and nothing small
    But is made fair with them.
They are the hands of living faith
    That touch the garment's hem.

They are as fair as bloom or air,
   They shine like any star,
And I am rich who learned from her
   How beautiful they are.

A LITTLE BOY IN THE MORNING

FRANCIS LEDWIDGE

He will not come, and still I wait.
He whistles at another gate
Where angels listen. Ah, I know
He will not come, yet if I go
How shall I know he did not pass
Barefooted in the flowery grass?

The moon leans on one silver horn
Above the silhouettes of morn,
And from their nest sills finches whistle
Or stooping pluck the downy thistle.
How is the morn so gay and fair
Without his whistling in the air?

The world is calling, I must go.
How shall I know he did not pass
Barefooted in the shining grass?

HOUSEHOLD GODS

J. H. MacNair

The baby takes to her bed at night
A one-eyed rabbit that once was white;
A watch that came from a cracker, I think;
And a lidless inkpot that never held ink.
And the secret is locked in the tiny breast
Of why she loves these and leaves the rest.

And I give a loving glance as I go
To three brass pots on a shelf in a row;
To my grandfather's grandfather's loving-cup,
And a bandy-legged chair I once picked up.
And I can't, for the life of me, make you see
Why just these things are a part of me!

MARY SETS THE TABLE[1]

David Morton

She brings such gay and shining things to pass,
  With delicate, deft fingers that are learned
In ways of silverware and cup and glass,
  Arrayed in ordered patterns, trimly turned; —
And never guesses how this subtle ease
  Is older than the oldest tale we tell,
This gift that guides her through such tricks as these, —
  And my delight in watching her, as well.

[1] From "Ships in Harbour," by David Morton. Courtesy of G. P.
Putnam's Sons, Publishers, New York and London.

She thinks not how this art with spoon and plate,
   Is one with ancient women baking bread:
An epic heritance come down of late
   To slender hands, and dear, delightful head,—
How Trojan housewives vie in serving me,
Where Mary sets the table things for tea.

A CHARM[1]

CHRISTOPHER MORLEY

O wood, burn bright; O flame, be quick;
   O smoke, draw cleanly up the flue—
My lady chose your every brick
   And sets her dearest hopes on you!

Logs cannot burn, nor tea be sweet,
   Nor white bread turn to crispy toast,
Until your charm be made complete
   By love, to lay the sooty ghost.

And then, dear books, dear waiting chairs,
   Dear china and mahogany,
Draw close, for on the happy stairs
   My brown-eyed girl comes down for tea!

THE SHADOW PEOPLE

FRANCIS LEDWIDGE

Old lame Bridget doesn't hear
Fairy music in the grass
When the gloaming's on the mere
And the shadow people pass.
Never hears their slow gray feet
Coming from the village street
Just beyond the parson's wall,
Where the clover globes are sweet
And the mushroom's parasol
Opens in the moonlit rain.
Every night I hear them call
From their long and merry train.
Old lame Bridget says to me,
"It is just your fancy, child."
She cannot believe I see
Laughing faces in the wild,
Hands that twinkle in the sedge
Bowing at the water's edge
Where the finny minnows quiver,
Shaping on a blue wave's ledge
Bubble foam to sail the river.
And the sunny hands to me
Beckon ever, beckon ever.
Oh! I would be wild and free
And with the shadow people be.

A FAIRY TALE

AUSTIN DOBSON

"On court, hélas! après la vérité;
Ah! croyez-moi, l'erreur a son mérite."
                                        VOLTAIRE

Curled in a maze of dolls and bricks,
I find Miss Mary, *aetat* six,
    Blonde, blue-eyed, frank, capricious,
Absorbed in her first fairy book,
From which she scarce can pause to look,
    Because it's "*so* delicious!"

"Such marvels, too. A wondrous Boat,
In which they cross a magic Moat,
    That's smooth as glass to row on—
A Cat that brings all kinds of things;
And see, the Queen has angel wings—
    Then OGRE comes"—and so on.

What trash it is! How sad to find
(Dear Moralist!) the childish mind,
    So active and so pliant,
Rejecting themes in which you mix
Fond truths with pleasing facts, to fix
    On tales of Dwarf and Giant!

In merest prudence men should teach
That cats mellifluous in speech
    Are painful contradictions;

That science ranks as monstrous things
Two pairs of upper limbs; so wings—
  E'en angels' wings!—are fictions;

That there's no giant now but Steam;
That life, although "an empty dream,"
  Is scarce a "land of Fairy."
"Of course I said all this?" Why, no,
I *did* a thing far wiser, though,—
  I read the tale with Mary.

WITH A FIRST READER

Rupert Hughes

Dear little child, this little book
  Is less a primer than a key
To sunder gates where wonder waits
  Your "Open Sesame!"

These tiny syllables look large;
  They'll fret your wide, bewildered eyes;
But "Is the cat upon the mat?"
  Is passport to the skies.

For yet awhile, and you shall turn
  From Mother Goose to Avon's swan;
From Mary's lamb to grim Khayyam,
  And Mancha's mad-wise Don.

You'll writhe at Jean Valjean's disgrace;
  And D'Artagnan and Ivanhoe
Shall steal your sleep; and you shall weep
  At Sidney Carton's woe.

You'll find old Chaucer young once more,
  Beaumont and Fletcher fierce with fire;
At your demand, John Milton's hand
  Shall wake his ivory lyre.

And learning other tongues, you'll learn
  All times are one; all men, one race;
Hear Homer speak, as Greek to Greek;
  See Dante, face to face.

Arma virumque shall resound;
  And Horace wreathe his rhymes afresh;
You'll rediscover Laura's lover;
  Meet Gretchen in the flesh.

Oh, could I find for the first time
  The Churchyard Elegy again!
Retaste the sweets of new-found Keats;
  Read Byron now as then!

Make haste to wander these old roads,
  O envied little parvenue;
For all things trite shall leap alight
  And bloom again for you!

THE SCHOOL BOY READS HIS ILIAD[1]

David Morton

The sounding battles leave him nodding still:
  The din of javelins at the distant wall
Is far too faint to wake that weary will
  That all but sleeps for cities where they fall.
He cares not if this Helen's face were fair,
  Nor if the thousand ships shall go or stay;
In vain the rumbling chariots throng the air
  With sounds the centuries shall not hush away.

Beyond the window where the Spring is new,
  Are marbles in a square, and tops again,
And floating voices tell him what they do,
  Luring his thoughts from these long-warring men,—
And though the camp be visited with gods,
He dreams of marbles and of tops, and nods.

OLD SUSAN

Walter de la Mare

When Susan's work was done, she'd sit
With one fat guttering candle lit,
And window opened wide to win
The sweet night air to enter in;
There, with a thumb to keep her place
She'd read, with stern and wrinkled face.

[1] From "Ships in Harbour," by David Morton. Courtesy of G. P. Putnam's Sons, Publishers, New York and London.

Her mild eyes gliding very slow
Across the letters to and fro,
While wagged the guttering candle flame
In the wind that through the window came.
And sometimes in the silence she
Would mumble a sentence audibly,
Or shake her head as if to say,
"You silly souls, to act this way!"
And never a sound from night I'd hear,
Unless some far-off cock crowed clear;
Or her old shuffling thumb should turn
Another page; and rapt and stern,
Through her great glasses bent on me
She'd glance into reality;
And shake her round old silvery head,
With—"You!—I thought you was in bed!"—
Only to tilt her book again,
And rooted in Romance remain.

LITTLE BATEESE[1]

WILLIAM HENRY DRUMMOND

You bad leetle boy, not moche you care
How busy you're kipin' your poor gran'père
   Tryin' to stop you ev'ry day
   Chasin' de hen aroun' de hay—
   W'y don't you geev' dem a chance to lay?
         Leetle Bateese!

[1] From "Johnnie Courteau," by William Henry Drummond. Courtesy of G. P. Putnam's Sons, Publishers, New York and London.

Off on de fiel' you foller de plough
Den w'en you're tire you scare de cow
  Sickin' de dog till dey jomp de wall
  So de milk ain't good for not'ing at all—
  An' you're only five an' a half dis fall,
             Leetle Bateese!

Too sleepy for sayin' de prayer to-night?
Never min'. I s'pose it'll be all right
  Say dem to-morrow—ah! dere he go!
  Fast asleep in a minute or so—
  An' he'll stay lak dat till de rooster crow,
             Leetle Bateese!

Den wake us up right away toute suite
Lookin' for somet'ing more to eat,
  Makin' me t'ink of dem long leg crane—
  Soon as dey swaller, dey start again;
  I wonder your stomach don't get no pain,
             Leetle Bateese!

But see heem now lyin' dere in bed,
Look at de arm onderneat' hees head;
  If he grow lak dat till he's twenty year
  I bet he'll be stronger dan Louis Cyr,
  An' beat all de voyageurs leevin' here,
             Leetle Bateese!

Jus' feel de muscle along hees back,
Won't geev' heem moche bodder for carry pack
  On de long portage, any size canoe;
  Dere's not many t'ing dat boy won't do,
  For he's got double-joint on hees body too,
             Leetle Bateese!

But leetle Bateese! please don't forget
We rader you're stayin' de small boy yet,
  So chase de chicken an' mak' dem scare
  An' do w'at you lak wit' your ole gran'père,
  For when you're beeg feller he won't be dere—
            Leetle Bateese!

THE GRAPEVINE SWING

Samuel Minturn Peck

When I was a boy on the old plantation,
  Down by the deep bayou,
The fairest spot of all creation,
  Under the arching blue;
When the wind came over the cotton and corn,
  To the long slim loop I'd spring
With brown feet bare, and hat-brim torn,
  And swing in the grapevine swing.

Swinging in the grapevine swing,
Laughing where the wild birds sing,
  I dream and sigh
  For the days gone by,
Swinging in the grapevine swing.

Out—o'er the water-lilies bonny and bright,
  Back—to the moss-grown trees;
I shouted and sang with a heart as light
  As a wild rose tossed by the breeze.
The mocking-bird joined in my careless glee,
  I longed for no angel's wing,
I was just as near heaven as I wanted to be
Swinging in the grapevine swing.

Swinging in the grapevine swing,
Laughing where the wild birds sing,—
  Oh, to be a boy
  With a heart full of joy,
Swinging in the grapevine swing.

I'm weary at noon, I'm weary at night,
  I'm fretted and sore of heart,
And care is sowing my locks with white
  As I wend through the fevered mart.
I'm tired of the world with its pride and pomp,
  And fame seems a worthless thing.
I'd barter it all for one day's romp,
  And a swing in the grapevine swing.

Swinging in the grapevine swing,
Laughing where the wild birds sing,
  I would I were away
  From the world to-day,
Swinging in the grapevine swing.

WE MEET AT MORN

HARDWICKE DRUMMOND RAWNSLEY

Still half in dream, upon the stair I hear
A patter coming nearer, and more near,
And then upon my chamber door
A gentle tapping—
For dogs, though proud, are poor,
And if a tail will do to give command,
Why use a hand?
And after that a cry, half sneeze, half yapping,
And next a scuffle on the passage floor,

And then I know the creature lies to wait
Until the noiseless maid will lift the latch,
And like a spring
That gains its power by being tightly stayed,
The impatient thing
Into the room
Its whole glad heart doth fling.
And ere the gloom
Melts into light, and window blinds are rolled,
I hear a bounce upon the bed,
I feel a creeping toward me—a soft head,
And on my face
A tender nose, and cold—
That is the way, you know, that dogs embrace—
And on my hand, like sun-warmed rose-leaves flung,
The least faint flicker of the warmest tongue—
And so my dog and I have met and sworn
Fresh love and fealty for another morn.

"LADDIE"

KATHARINE LEE BATES

Lowly the soul that waits
At the white, celestial gates,
A threshold soul to greet
Belovéd feet.

Down the streets that are beams of sun
Cherubim children run;
They welcome it from the wall;
Their voices call.

But the Warder saith: "Nay, this
Is the City of Holy Bliss.
What claim canst thou make good
To angelhood?"

"Joy," answereth it from eyes
That are amber ecstasies,
Listening, alert, elate,
Before the gate.

> *Oh, how the frolic feet*
> *On lonely memory beat!*
> *What rapture in a run*
> *'Twixt snow and sun!*

"Nay, brother of the sod,
What part hast thou in God?
What spirit art thou of?"
It answers: "Love,"

Lifting its head, no less
Cajoling a caress,
Our winsome collie wraith,
Than in glad faith

The door will open wide,
Or kind voice bid: "Abide,
A threshold soul to greet
The longed-for feet."

> *Ah, Keeper of the Portal,*
> *If Love be not immortal,*
> *If Joy be not divine,*
> *What prayer is mine?*

TO MY CAT

ROSAMUND MARRIOTT WATSON

Half loving-kindliness and half disdain,
    Thou comest to my call serenely suave,
    With humming speech and gracious gesture grave,
In salutation courtly and urbane;
Yet must I humble me thy grace to gain,
    For wiles may win thee though no arts enslave,
    And nowhere gladly thou abidest save
Where naught disturbs the concord of thy reign.

Sphinx of my quiet hearth! who deign'st to dwell
    Friend of my toil, companion of mine ease,
    Thine is the lore of Ra and Rameses;
That men forget dost thou remember well,
    Beholden still in blinking reveries
With sombre, sea-green gaze inscrutable.

A FAITHFUL DOG

RICHARD BURTON

My merry-hearted comrade on a day
Gave over all his mirth, and went away
Upon the darksome journey I must face
Sometime as well. Each hour I miss his grace,
His meek obedience and his constancy.
Never again will he look up to me
With loyal eyes, nor leap for my caress
As one who wished not to be masterless;
And never shall I hear his pleading bark
Outside the door, when all the ways grow dark,

Bidding the housefolk gather close inside.
It seems a cruel thing, since he has died,
To make his memory small, or deem it sin
To reckon such a mate as less than kin.

O faithful follower, O gentle friend,
If thou art missing at the journey's end,
Whate'er of joy and solace there I find
Unshared by thee I left so far behind,
The gladness will be mixed with tears, I trow,
My little crony of the long ago!
For how could heaven be home-like, with the door
Fast-locked against a loved one, evermore?

A CHILD'S PET

WILLIAM HENRY DAVIES

When I sailed out of Baltimore,
    With twice a thousand head of sheep,
They would not eat, they would not drink,
    But bleated o'er the deep.

Inside the pens we crawled each day,
    To sort the living from the dead;
And when we reached the Mersey's mouth,
    Had lost five hundred head.

Yet every night and day one sheep,
    That had no fear of man or sea,
Stuck through the bars its pleading face,
    And it was stroked by me.

And to the sheep-men standing near,
  "You see," I said, "this one tame sheep?
It seems a child has lost her pet,
  And cried herself to sleep."

So every time we passed it by,
  Sailing to England's slaughter-house,
Eight ragged sheep-men—tramps and thieves—
  Would stroke that sheep's black nose.

THE DONKEY

Gilbert Keith Chesterton

When fishes flew and forests walked
  And figs grew upon thorn,
Some moment when the morn was blood
  Then surely I was born;

With monstrous head and sickening cry
  And ears like errant wings,
The devil's walking parody
  On all four-footed things.

The tattered outlaw of the earth,
  Of ancient crooked will;
Starve, scourge, deride me: I am dumb,
  I keep my secret still.

Fools! For I also had my hour;
  One far fierce hour and sweet:
There was a shout about my ears,
  And palms before my feet.

THE ROAD TO VAGABONDIA

DANA BURNET

He was sitting on the doorstep as I went strolling by;
A lonely little beggar with a wistful, homesick eye—
And he wasn't what you'd borrow, and he wasn't what you'd
steal,
But I guessed his heart was breaking, so I whistled him to
heel.

They had stoned him through the city streets, and naught the
city cared,
But I was heading outward, and the roads are sweeter shared,
So I took him for a comrade, and I whistled him away—
On the road to Vagabondia, that lies across the day!

Yellow dog he was; but bless you—he was just the chap for
me!
For I'd rather have an inch of dog than miles of pedigree.
So we stole away together, on the road that has no end,
With a new-coined day to fling away and all the stars to
spend!

Oh, to walk the road at morning, when the wind is blowing
clean,
And the yellow daisies fling their gold across a world of
green—
For the wind it heals the heartache, and the sun it dries the
scars,
On the road to Vagabondia that lies beneath the stars.

'Twas the wonder of our going cast a spell about our feet—
And we walked because the world was young, because the
    way was sweet;
And we slept in wild-rose meadows by the little wayside
    farms,
Till the Dawn came up the highroad with the dead moon in
    her arms.

Oh, the Dawn it went before us through a shining lane of skies,
And the Dream was at our heartstrings, and the Light was in
    our eyes,
And we made no boast of glory and we made no boast of
    birth,
On the road to Vagabondia that lies across the earth!

THE OXEN

Thomas Hardy

Christmas Eve, and twelve of the clock.
    "Now they are all on their knees,"
An elder said as we sat in a flock
    By the embers in hearthside ease.

We pictured the meek mild creatures where
    They dwelt in their strawy pen,
Nor did it occur to one of us there
    To doubt they were kneeling then.

So fair a fancy few would weave
    In these years! Yet, I feel
If someone said on Christmas Eve,
    "Come; see the oxen kneel

"In the lonely barton by yonder coomb
    Our childhood used to know,"
I should go with him in the gloom,
    Hoping it might be so.

THE OLD SWIMMIN'-HOLE[1]

James Whitcomb Riley

Oh! the old swimmin'-hole! whare the crick so still and deep
Looked like a baby-river that was laying half asleep,
And the gurgle of the worter round the drift jest below
Sounded like the laugh of something we onc't ust to know
Before we could remember anything but the eyes
Of the angels lookin' out as we left Paradise;
But the merry days of youth is beyond our controle,
And it's hard to part ferever with the old swimmin'-hole.

Oh! the old swimmin'-hole! In the happy days of yore,
When I ust to lean above it on the old sickamore,
Oh! it showed me a face in its warm sunny tide
That gazed back at me so gay and glorified,
It made me love myself, as I leaped to caress
My shadder smilin' up at me with sich tenderness.
But them days is past and gone, and old Time's tuck his toll
From the old man come back to the old swimmin'-hole.

Oh! the old swimmin'-hole! In the long, lazy days
When the hum-drum of school made so many run-a-ways,

[1] From "Morning," by James Whitcomb Riley. Copyright, 1907.
Used by special permission of the publishers, The Bobbs-Merrill
Company.

How plesant was the jurney down the old dusty lane,
Whare the tracks of our bare feet was all printed so plane
You could tell by the dent of the heel and the sole
They was lots o' fun on hands at the old swimmin'-hole.
But the lost joys is past! Let your tears in sorrow roll
Like the rain that ust to dapple up the old swimmin'-hole.

Thare the bullrushes growed, and the cattails so tall,
And the sunshine and shadder fell over it all;
And it mottled the worter with amber and gold
Tel the glad lilies rocked in the ripples that rolled;
And the snake-feeder's four gauzy wings fluttered by
Like the ghost of a daisy dropped out of the sky,
Or a wownded apple-blossom in the breeze's controle
As it cut acrost some orchurd to'rds the old swimmin'-hole.

Oh! the old swimmin'-hole! When I last saw the place,
The scenes was all changed, like the change in my face;
The bridge of the railroad now crosses the spot
Whare the old divin'-log lays sunk and fergot.
And I stray down the banks whare the trees ust to be—
But never again will theyr shade shelter me!
And I wish in my sorrow I could strip to the soul,
And dive off in my grave like the old swimmin'-hole.

LIFE IN THE OPEN

"AND THE WHEEL'S KICK AND THE WIND'S SONG AND THE WHITE SAIL'S SHAKING" (PAGE 93)

TEWKESBURY ROAD[1]

John Masefield

It is good to be out on the road, and going one knows not
    where,
    Going through meadow and village, one knows not whither
    nor why;
Through the grey light drift of the dust, in the keen cool rush
    of the air,
    Under the flying white clouds, and the broad blue lift of
    the sky.

And to halt at the chattering brook, in the tall green fern at
    the brink
    Where the harebell grows, and the gorse, and the foxgloves
    purple and white;
Where the shy-eyed delicate deer troop down to the brook to
    drink
    When the stars are mellow and large at the coming on of
    the night.

O, to feel the beat of the rain, and the homely smell of the
    earth,
    Is a tune for the blood to jig to, a joy past power of words;
And the blessed green comely meadows are all a-ripple with
    mirth
    At the noise of the lambs at play and the dear wild cry of
    the birds.

[1] Reprinted from John Masefield's "Salt-Water Ballads." By special
arrangement with The Macmillan Company, Publishers.

WANDER–THIRST

GERALD GOULD

Beyond the East the sunrise; beyond the West the sea,
And East and West the wander-thirst that will not let me be;
It works in me like madness, dear, to bid me say good-bye;
For the seas call and the stars call, and oh! the call of
the sky.

I know not where the white road runs, nor what the blue
hills are,
But a man can have the Sun for friend, and for his guide
a star;
And there's no end of voyaging when once the voice is heard,
For the river calls and the road calls, and oh! the call of
a bird!

Yonder the long horizon lies, and there by night and day
The old ships draw to home again, the young ships sail away;
And come I may, but go I must, and, if men ask you why,
You may put the blame on the Stars and the Sun and the
white road and the sky.

THE GYPSY HEART

HARRY NOYES PRATT

When I was just a tiny chap
Long years ago, they say
The gypsies rode away with me
Across the sunlit day;

Across the moor of yellow furze,
  Out through the day, beyond
The purpling of the distant hills;
  With me, a vagabond.

We loitered lazy on the road
  That led afar from town.
We made the gypsy patteran
  For those who followed down.
The wind that came across the moor
  Blew salty from the sea;
The stars above the drowsy stream
  Smiled friendly down on me.

Through summer days we rode and far,
  And far the free road ran;
But every road must find an end,
  And every caravan
Must creak and pause and roll to rest
  When summer days have gone—
And so they brought me home again
  And left me in the dawn.

The brick-walled days that hold me here
  Run wearily and slow;
The sun is like a brazen ball
  With brazen streets below.
I smell the gorse upon the moor,
  And winds from off the sea—
The gypsies stole my heart, and gave
  A gypsy heart to me.

THE REMEDY

HARRY KEMP

When you've failed with ordered people, when you've sunk
    neck-deep again
In the sluggish wash and jetsam of the sluggish tides of men,
Don't get old and mean and bitter,—there's a primal remedy,
Just take a ship to sea, my lad, just take a ship to sea.

There are shipmen grey and agèd but still full of ancient
    mirth,
And they drew their joy of living, not from rooting in
    the earth,
But from sticking out forever with a sail that's never furled
And by seeing all the oceans and the wonders of the world;
In the dim Phœnician days and in the wild sea-times of old
Do you think they only voyaged for the red of shining gold?
No, they slipped beyond the sky-line, for they felt it good to
    be
On a ship that tramped with thunder down the highways of
    the sea.

When you've drunk the lees of failure, when you've fought
    and never won,
When you've cursed the stale recurrence of the certain,
    weary sun,
And the daily, fruitless struggle pledging youth for usury,
Come, and cast the world behind you, and take ship for open
    sea;
All you need will be your dunnage and your knife upon your
    hip,
And you'll find a bunk that waits you in the fo'c'sle of a ship,

And you'll find the wind about you and the everlasting sky
Leaning huge from four horizons as the flying scud blows
    by—
And you'll find the ancient healing, ever waiting, ever free,
That all men have found forever in the sailing of the sea.

THE WILDERNESS

Edwin Arlington Robinson

Come away! come away! there's a frost along the marshes,
And a frozen wind that skims the shoal where it shakes the
    dead black water;
There's a moan across the lowland and a wailing through the
    woodland
Of a dirge that sings to send us back to the arms of those that
    love us.
There is nothing left but ashes now where the crimson chills
    of autumn
Put off the summer's languor with a touch that made us glad
For the glory that is gone from us, with a flight we cannot
    follow,
To the slopes of other valleys and the sounds of other shores.

Come away! come away! you can hear them calling, calling,
Calling us to come to them, and roam no more.
Over there beyond the ridges and the land that lies between
    us,
There's an old song calling us to come!

Come away! come away!—for the scenes we leave behind us
Are barren for the lights of home and a flame that's young
    forever;

And the lonely trees around us creak the warning of the nightwind,
That love and all the dreams of love are away beyond the mountains.
The songs that call for us to-night, they have called for men before us,
And the winds that blow the message, they have blown ten thousand years;
But this will end our wander-time, for we know the joy that waits us
In the strangeness of home-coming, and a woman's waiting eyes.

Come away! come away! there is nothing now to cheer us—
Nothing now to comfort us, but love's road home:—
Over there beyond the darkness there's a window gleams to greet us,
And a warm hearth waits for us within.

Come away! come away!—or the roving-fiend will hold us,
And make us all to dwell with him to the end of human faring:
There are no men yet may leave him when his hands are clutched upon them,
There are none will own his enmity, there are none will call him brother.
So we'll be up and on the way, and the less we boast the better
For the freedom that God gave us and the dread we do not know:—
The frost that skips the willow-leaf will again be back to blight it,
And the doom we cannot fly from is the doom we do not see.

Come away! come away! there are dead men all around
us—
Frozen men that mock us with a wild, hard laugh
That shrieks and sinks and whimpers in the shrill November
rushes
And the long fall wind on the lake.

THE SONG MY PADDLE SINGS

E. Pauline Johnson

West wind, blow from your prairie nest,
Blow from the mountains, blow from the west.
The sail is idle, the sailor too;
O wind of the west, we wait for you!
Blow, blow!
I have wooed you so,
But never a favour you bestow.
You rock your cradle the hills between,
But scorn to notice my white lateen.

I stow the sail, unship the mast;
I wooed thee long, but my wooing's past;
My paddle will lull you into rest.
O drowsy wind of the drowsy west,
Sleep, sleep,
By your mountain steep,
Or down where the prairie grasses sweep!
Now fold in slumber your laggard wings,
For soft is the song my paddle sings.

August is laughing across the sky,
Laughing while paddle, canoe, and I

Drift, drift,
Where the hills uplift
On either side of the current swift.

The river rolls in its rocky bed;
My paddle is plying its way ahead;
Dip, dip,
When the waters flip
In foam as over their breast we slip.

And oh, the river runs swifter now;
The eddies circle about my bow!
Swirl, swirl!
How the ripples curl
In many a dangerous pool awhirl!

And forward far the rapids roar,
Fretting their margin for evermore;
Dash, dash,
With a mighty crash,
They seethe, and boil, and bound, and splash.

Be strong, O paddle! be brave, canoe!
The reckless waves you must plunge into.
Reel, reel,
On your trembling keel—
But never a fear my craft will feel.

We've raced the rapid; we're far ahead!
The river slips through its silent bed.
Sway, sway,
As the bubbles spray
And fall in tinkling tunes away.

And up on the hills against the sky,
A fir tree rocking its lullaby,
Swings, swings,
Its emerald wings,
Swelling the song that my paddle sings.

SEA–FEVER[1]

John Masefield

I must go down to the seas again, to the lonely sea and the
    sky,
And all I ask is a tall ship and a star to steer her by,
And the wheel's kick and the wind's song and the white sail's
    shaking,
And a grey mist on the sea's face, and a grey dawn breaking.

I must go down to the seas again, for the call of the running
    tide
Is a wild call and a clear call that may not be denied;
And all I ask is a windy day with the white clouds flying,
And the flung spray and the blown spume, and the sea-gulls
    crying.

I must go down to the seas again, to the vagrant gypsy life,
To the gull's way and the whale's way where the wind's like
    a whetted knife;
And all I ask is a merry yarn from a laughing fellow-rover,
And quiet sleep and a sweet dream when the long trick's over.

[1] Reprinted from John Masefield's "Collected Poems." By special
arrangement with The Macmillan Company, Publishers.

OLD GREY SQUIRREL

Alfred Noyes

A great while ago, there was a school-boy.
   He lived in a cottage by the sea.
And the very first thing he could remember
   Was the rigging of the schooners by the quay.

He could watch them, when he woke, from his window,
   With the tall cranes hoisting out the freight.
And he used to think of shipping as a sea-cook,
   And sailing to the Golden Gate.

For he used to buy the yellow penny-dreadfuls,
   And read them where he fished for conger eels,
And listened to the lapping of the water,
   The green and oily water round the keels.

There were trawlers with their shark-mouthed flat-fish,
   And red nets hanging out to dry,
And the skate the skipper kept because he liked 'em,
   And landsmen never knew the fish to fry.

There were brigantines with timber out of Norroway,
   Oozing with the syrups of the pine.
There were rusty dusty schooners out of Sunderland,
   And ships of the Blue Cross Line.

And to tumble down a hatch into a cabin
   Was better than the best of broken rules;
For the smell of 'em was like a Christmas dinner,
   And the feel of 'em was like a box of tools.

And, before he went to sleep in the evening,
   The very last thing that he could see
Was the sailor-men a-dancing in the moonlight
   By the capstan that stood upon the quay.

He is perched upon a high stool in London.
   The Golden Gate is very far away.
They caught him, and they caged him, like a squirrel.
   He is totting up accounts, and going grey.

He will never, never, never, sail to 'Frisco.
   But the very last thing that he will see
Will be sailor-men a-dancing in the sunrise
   By the capstan that stands upon the quay. . . .

To the tune of an old concertina,
   By the capstan that stands upon the quay.

THE SEA GYPSY

RICHARD HOVEY

I am fevered with the sunset,
   I am fretful with the bay,
For the wander-thirst is on me
   And my soul is in Cathay.

There's a schooner in the offing,
   With her topsails shot with fire,
And my heart has gone aboard her
   For the Islands of Desire.

I must forth again to-morrow!
  With the sunset I must be
Hull down on the trail of rapture
  In the wonder of the sea.

SNOWSHOEING SONG

Arthur Weir

Hilloo, hilloo, hilloo, hilloo!
Gather, gather, ye men in white;
The winds blow keenly, the moon is bright,
The sparkling snow lies firm and white;
Tie on the shoes, no time to lose,
We must be over the hill to-night.

Hilloo, hilloo, hilloo, hilloo!
Swiftly in single file we go,
The city is soon left far below,
Its countless lights like diamonds glow;
And as we climb we hear the chime
Of church bells stealing o'er the snow.

Hilloo, hilloo, hilloo, hilloo!
Like winding sheet about the dead,
O'er hill and dale the snow is spread,
And silences our hurried tread;
The pines bend low, and to and fro
The maples toss their boughs o'erhead.

Hilloo, hilloo, hilloo, hilloo!
We laugh to scorn the angry blast,
The mountain top is gained and past,
Descent begins, 'tis ever fast—
One short quick run, and toil is done,
We reach the welcome inn at last.

Shake off, shake off the clinging snow;
Unloose the shoe, the sash untie,
Fling tuque and mittens lightly by;
The chimney fire is blazing high,
And, richly stored, the festive board
Awaits the merry company.

Remove the fragments of the feast!
The steaming coffee, waiter, bring.
Now tell the tale, the chorus sing,
And let the laughter loudly ring;
Here's to our host, drink down the toast,
Then up! for time is on the wing.

Hilloo, hilloo, hilloo, hilloo!
The moon is sinking out of sight,
Across the sky dark clouds take flight,
And dimly looms the mountain height;
Tie on the shoes, no time to lose,
We must be home again to-night.

TROUT–FISHING ON TWEED

Andrew Lang

As birds are fain to build their nest
   The first soft sunny day,
So longing wakens in my breast
   A month before the May,
When now the wind is from the West,
   And Winter melts away.

The snow lies yet on Eildon Hill,
   And soft the breezes blow.
If melting snows the waters fill,
   We nothing heed the snow,
But we must up and take our will,—
   A-fishing we will go!

Below the branches brown and bare,
   Beneath the primrose lea,
The trout lies waiting for his fare,
   A happy trout is he;
He's hooked and springs and splashes there
   Like salmon from the sea!

Oh, April tide's a pleasant tide,
   However times may fall,
And sweet to welcome Spring, the Bride,
   You hear the mavis call;
But all adown the water-side
   The Spring's most fair of all.

CADENCES

Samuel T. Clover

I am riding, riding, riding, on the hard dirt road,
And my horse's ears are pointed, and my horse's neck is
    bowed.
For in his veins pulsating is the ichor of the spring,
And I catch the lilt of music his dancing hoofbeats ring:

It's "Good-to-be-alive! Good-to-be-alive! Good-to-be-alive
    to-day!
What-fun-it-is! What-fun-it-is!" they seem to me to say;
And in the saddle, marking time, I fervently repeat,
"I-love-it-too! I-love-it-too!" with every rhythmic beat.

Thus on we go together, my eager horse and I,
In tune with one another and a California sky!
Intoxication's in the air, for blossoming orchards shed
The fragrance of their subtleties about the rider's head.

Clippity-clip! Clippity-clip! the hoofbeats strike the ground,
But more than that the message I gather from the sound;
I get from it the thrill of joy so bounteously bestowed,
When I am in the saddle on the hard dirt road.

PARDS

Hugh J. Hughes

So—good-by! The dreamy splendor of the mornings
   Breaking over yonder range shall call you back;
Dusk and dawn and night and noon be filled with yearnings
   For the cattle-trail, the rough and ample shack.

So—good-by! Before your face the East is lying,
   Old and worn, and haggard with a thousand woes.
Ah! you'll long to sit again a-saddle, flying
   Past the dawn-dew, the odor of the rose!

When the mother calls, we question not, but answer,
   And the mother East is calling you, I know;
But above the dancers' music and the dancer
   You'll be hearing songs the Eastmen never knew—

Songs that dripped their wordless music down the starry
   Nights we've rode the range together, you and I;
Thoughts so fragile you would scarcely think they'd carry
   Over all the days and miles that interlie!

There will come to you, like lovers, softly gliding
   Into all your thousand doings and your dreams,
The camp-song, the round-up, the riding,
   The wolf's howl, the brawling of the streams.

So—good-by! Loose the bronco from his tether;
   He'll be ready, and you'll want him by and by;
'Twill be sunny heart, and song, and ranchers' weather
   When we ride the range together, you and I!

THE COWBOY'S LIFE

Attributed to JAMES BARTON ADAMS

The bawl of a steer,
To a cowboy's ear,
   Is music of sweetest strain;
And the yelping notes
Of the grey coyotes
   To him are a glad refrain.

And his jolly song
Speeds him along,
   As he thinks of the little gal
With golden hair
Who is waiting there
   At the bars of the home corral.

For a kingly crown
In the noisy town
   His saddle he wouldn't change;
No life so free
As the life we see
   'Way out on the Yaso range.

His eyes are bright,
And his heart as light
   As the smoke of his cigarette;
There's never a care
For his soul to bear,
   No trouble to make him fret.

The rapid beat
Of his broncho's feet
    On the sod as he speeds along,
Keeps living time
To the ringing rhyme
    Of his rollicking cowboy song.

Hike it, cowboys,
For the range away
    On the back of a bronc of steel,
With a careless flirt
Of the rawhide quirt
    And the dig of a roweled heel!

The winds may blow
And the thunder growl
    Or the breezes may safely moan;—
A cowboy's life
Is the royal life,
    His saddle his kingly throne.

Saddle up, boys,
For the work is play
    When love's in the cowboy's eyes,—
When his heart is light
As the clouds of white
    That swim in the summer skies.

THE HILLS[1]

Berton Braley

Partner, remember the hills?
The gray, barren, bleak old hills
We know so well—
Not those gentle, placid slopes that swell
In lazy undulations, lush and green.
No; the real hills, the jagged crests,
The sharp and sheer-cut pinnacles of earth
That stand against the azure—gaunt, serene,
Careless of all our little worsts and bests,
Our sorrow and our mirth!

Partner, remember the hills?
Those snow-crowned, granite battlements of hills
We loved of old.
They stood so calm, inscrutable and cold,
Somehow it never seemed they cared at all
For you or me, our fortunes or our fall,
And yet we felt their thrall;
And ever and forever to the end
We shall not cease, my friend,
To hear their call.

Partner, remember the hills?
The grim and massive majesty of hills
That soared so far,
Seeming, at night, to scrape against a star.

[1] From "Songs of the Workaday World," by Berton Braley. Copyright, 1915, by George H. Doran Company, Publishers.

Do you remember how we lay at night
(When the great herd had settled down to sleep)
And watched the moonshine—white
Against the peaks all garlanded with snow,
While soft and low
The night wind murmured in our ears—and so
We wrapped our blankets closer, looked again
At those great shadowy mountain-tops, and then
Sank gently to our deep
And quiet sleep?

Partner, remember the hills?
The real hills, the true hills.
Ah, I have tried
To brush the memory of them aside;
To learn to love
Those fresh, green hills the poets carol of;
But the old gray hills of barrenness still hold
My heart so much in thrall
That I forget the beauty all about,
The grass and flowers and all;
And just cry out
To take again the faint and wind-swept trail,
To see my naked mountains, shale and snow,
To feel again the hill-wind and to know
The spell that shall not fail.

HILLS

ARTHUR GUITERMAN

I never loved your plains!—
　　Your gentle valleys,
Your drowsy country lanes
　　And pleachèd alleys.

I want my hills!—the trail
　　That scorns the hollow.—
Up, up the rugged shale
　　Where few will follow.

Up, over wooded crest
　　And mossy boulder,
With strong thigh, heaving chest,
　　And swinging shoulder,

So let me hold my way,
　　By nothing halted,
Until, at close of day,
　　I stand, exalted,

High on my hills of dream—
　　Dear hills that know me!
And then, how fair will seem
　　The lands below me!

How pure, at vesper-time,
　　The far bells chiming!
God, give me hills to climb,
　　And strength for climbing!

THE JOY OF THE HILLS

EDWIN MARKHAM

I ride on the mountain tops, I ride;
I have found my life and am satisfied.
Onward I ride in the blowing oats,
Checking the field-lark's rippling notes—
      Lightly I sweep
      From steep to steep:
Over my head through the branches high
Come glimpses of a rushing sky;
The tall oats brush my horse's flanks;
Wild poppies crowd on the sunny banks;
A bee booms out the scented grass;
A jay laughs with me as I pass.

I ride on the hills, I forgive, I forget
      Life's hoard of regret—
      All the terror and pain
      Of the chafing chain.
      Grind on, O cities, grind:
      I leave you a blur behind.
I am lifted elate—the skies expand:
Here the world's heaped gold is a pile of sand.
Let them weary and work in their narrow walls:
I ride with the voices of waterfalls!

I swing on as one in a dream—I swing
Down the airy hollows, I shout, I sing!
The world is gone like an empty word:
My body's a bough in the wind, my heart a bird!

THE LITTLE SHEPHERD'S SONG

Thirteenth Century

WILLIAM ALEXANDER PERCY

The leaves, the little birds, and I,
The fleece clouds and the sweet, sweet sky,
The pages singing as they ride
Down there, down there where the river is wide—
Heigh-ho, what a day! What a lovely day!
Even too lovely to hop and play
    With my sheep,
        Or sleep
    In the sun!

And so I lie in the deep, deep grass
And watch the pages as they pass,
And sing to them as they to me
Till they turn the bend by the poplar tree.
And then—O then I sing right on
To the leaves and the lambs and myself alone!
    For I think there must be
        Inside of me
           A bird!

"CLEAR AND GENTLE STREAM"

ROBERT BRIDGES

Clear and gentle stream!
Known and loved so long
That hast heard the song,
And the idle dream
Of my boyish day;

While I once again
Down thy margin stray,
In the selfsame strain
Still my voice is spent,
With my old lament
And my idle dream,
Clear and gentle stream!

Where my old seat was
Here again I sit,
Where the old boughs knit
Over stream and grass
A translucent eaves;
Where back eddies play
Shipwreck with the leaves,
And the proud swans stray,
Sailing one by one
Out of stream and sun,
And the fish lie cool
In their chosen pool.

Many an afternoon
Of the summer day
Dreaming here I lay;
And I know how soon,
Idly at its hour,
First the deep bell hums
From the minster tower,
And then evening comes,
Creeping up the glade,
With her lengthening shade,
And the tardy boon,
Of her brightening moon.

Clear and gentle stream!
Ere again I go
Where thou dost not flow,
Well does it beseem
Thee to hear again
Once my youthful song,
That familiar strain
Silent now so long:
Be as I content
With my old lament
And my idle dream,
Clear and gentle stream.

MORNING IN CAMP

HERBERT BASHFORD

A bed of ashes and a half-burned brand
  Now mark the spot where last night's campfire sprung
  And licked the dark with slender scarlet tongue;
The sea draws back from shores of yellow sand,
Nor speaks lest he awake the sleeping land;
  Tall trees grow out of shadows; high among
  Their somber boughs one clear, sweet song is sung;
In deep ravine by drooping cedars spanned
All drowned in glory, a flying pheasant's whir
  Rends morning's solemn hush; gray rabbits run
    Across the covered glade; then far away
Upon a hill, each huge, expectant fir
  Holds open arms in welcome to the sun,—
    Great pulsing heart of bold advancing day.

A VAGABOND SONG

Bliss Carman

There is something in the autumn that is native to my
blood—
Touch of manner, hint of mood;
And my heart is like a rhyme,
With the yellow and the purple and the crimson keeping time.

The scarlet of the maples can shake me like a cry
Of bugles going by.
And my lonely spirit thrills
To see the frosty asters like a smoke upon the hills.

There is something in October sets the gipsy blood astir;
We must rise and follow her,
When from every hill of flame
She calls and calls each vagabond by name.

THE TRAVELLER[1]

Cicely Fox Smith

I've loops o' string in the place of buttons, I've mostly holes
for a shirt;
My boots are bust and my hat's a goner, I'm gritty with dust
and dirt;
An' I'm sitting here on a bollard watchin' the China ships go
forth,
Seein' the black little tugs come slidin' with timber booms
from the North,

[1] From "Sailor Town," by Cicely Fox Smith. Copyright, 1918, by
George H. Doran Company, Publishers.

Sittin' and seein' the broad Pacific break at my feet in foam....
Me that was born with a taste for travel in a back alley at
      home.

They put me to school when I was a nipper at the Board
      School down in the slums,
An' some of the kids was good at spellin' and some at figures
      and sums;
And whether I went or whether I didn't they learned me
      nothin' at all,
Only I'd watch the flies go walkin' over the maps on the wall,
Strollin' over the lakes an' mountains, over the plains an'
      sea,—
As if they was born with a taste for travel . . . somethin' the
      same as me!

If I'd been born a rich man's youngster with lots o' money to
      burn,
It wouldn't ha' gone in marble mansions and statues at every
      turn,
It wouldn't ha' gone in wine and women, or dogs an' horses
      an' play,
Nor yet in collectin' bricks an' bracks in a harmless kind of
      a way;
I'd ha' paid my fare where I've beat my way (but I couldn't
      ha' liked it more!),
Me that was born with a taste for travel—the same if you're
      rich or poor.

I'd ha' gone bowlin' in yachts and rollin' in plush-padded
      Pullman cars,—
The same as I've seen 'em when I lay restin' at night-time
      under the stars,

Me that have beat the ties and rode the bumpers from sea to
    sea,
Me that have sweated in stokeholds and dined of mouldy
    salt-horse and tea,
Me that have melted like grease at Perim and froze like
    boards off the Horn,
All along of a taste for travel that was in me when I was born.

I ain't got folks an' I ain't got money, I ain't got nothin' at
    all,
But a sort of a queer old thirst that keeps me movin' on till I
    fall,
And many a time I've been short o' shelter and many a time
    o' grub,
But I've got away from the rows o' houses, the streets, an'
    the corner pub—
And here by the side of a sea that's shinin' under a sky like
    flame,
Me that was born with a taste for travel, give thanks because
    o' the same.

THE BEST ROAD OF ALL

CHARLES HANSON TOWNE

I like a road that leads away to prospects white and fair,
A road that is an ordered road, like a nun's evening prayer;
But, best of all, I love a road that leads to God knows where.

You come upon it suddenly—you cannot seek it out;
It's like a secret still unheard and never noised about;
But when you see it, gone at once is every lurking doubt.

It winds beside some rushing stream where aspens lightly
    quiver;
It follows many a broken field by many a shining river;
It seems to lead you on and on, forever and forever!

You tramp along its dusty way, beneath its shadowy trees,
And hear beside you chattering birds or happy booming bees,
And all around you golden sounds, the green leaves' litanies.

And here's a hedge, and there's a cot; and then—strange,
    sudden turns;
A dip, a rise, a little glimpse where the red sunset burns;
A bit of sky at evening time, the scent of hidden ferns.

A winding road, a loitering road, a finger-mark of God
Traced when the Maker of the world leaned over ways
    untrod.
See! Here He smiled His glowing smile, and lo, the golden-
    rod!

I like a road that wanders straight; the King's highway is
    fair,
And lovely are the sheltered lanes that take you here and
    there;
But, best of all, I love a road that leads to God knows where.

SOCIAL IDEALS AND PROBLEMS

"AT THE GATE OF THE WEST I STAND" (PAGE 127)

WORK

Angela Morgan

A SONG OF TRIUMPH

Work!
Thank God for the might of it,
The ardor, the urge, the delight of it—
Work that springs from the heart's desire,
Setting the brain and the soul on fire—
Oh, what is so good as the heat of it,
And what is so glad as the beat of it,
And what is so kind as the stern command,
Challenging brain and heart and hand?

Work!
Thank God for the pride of it,
For the beautiful, conquering tide of it,
Sweeping the life in its furious flood,
Thrilling the arteries, cleansing the blood,
Mastering stupor and dull despair,
Moving the dreamer to do and dare.
Oh, what is so good as the urge of it,
And what is so glad as the surge of it,
And what is so strong as the summons deep,
Rousing the torpid soul from sleep?

Work!
Thank God for the pace of it,
For the terrible, keen, swift race of it;

Fiery steeds in full control,
Nostrils a-quiver to meet the goal.
Work, the Power that drives behind,
Guiding the purposes, taming the mind,
Holding the runaway wishes back,
Reining the will to one steady track,
Speeding the energies faster, faster,
Triumphing over disaster.
Oh, what is so good as the pain of it,
And what is so great as the gain of it?
And what is so kind as the cruel goad,
Forcing us on through the rugged road?

Work!
Thank God for the swing of it,
For the clamoring, hammering ring of it,
Passion of labor daily hurled
On the mighty anvils of the world.
Oh, what is so fierce as the flame of it?
And what is so huge as the aim of it?
Thundering on through dearth and doubt,
Calling the plan of the Maker out.
Work, the Titan; Work, the friend,
Shaping the earth to a glorious end,
Draining the swamps and blasting the hills,
Doing whatever the Spirit wills—
Rending a continent apart,
To answer the dream of the Master heart.
Thank God for a world where none may shirk—
Thank God for the splendor of work!

WORK

HENRY VAN DYKE

Let me but do my work from day to day,
  In field or forest, at the desk or loom,
  In roaring market-place or tranquil room;
Let me but find it in my heart to say,
When vagrant wishes beckon me astray,
  "This is my work; my blessing, not my doom;
  Of all who live, I am the one by whom
This work can best be done in the right way."

Then shall I see it not too great, nor small,
  To suit my spirit and to prove my powers;
  Then shall I cheerful greet the laboring hours,
And cheerful turn, when the long shadows fall
At eventide, to play and love and rest,
Because I know for me my work is best.

MENDING WALL

ROBERT FROST

Something there is that doesn't love a wall,
That sends the frozen-ground-swell under it,
And spills the upper boulders in the sun;
And makes gaps even two can pass abreast.
The work of hunters is another thing:
I have come after them and made repair
Where they have left not one stone on a stone,
But they would have the rabbit out of hiding,
To please the yelping dogs. The gaps I mean,

No one has seen them made or heard them made,
But at spring mending-time we find them there.
I let my neighbor know beyond the hill;
And on a day we meet to walk the line
And set the wall between us once again.
We keep the wall between us as we go.
To each the boulders that have fallen to each.
And some are loaves and some so nearly balls
We have to use a spell to make them balance:
"Stay where you are until our backs are turned!"
We wear our fingers rough with handling them.
Oh, just another kind of out-door game,
One on a side. It comes to little more:
There where it is we do not need the wall:
He is all pine and I am apple orchard.
My apple trees will never get across
And eat the cones under his pines, I tell him.
He only says, "Good fences make good neighbors."
Spring is the mischief in me, and I wonder
If I could put a notion in his head:
"*Why* do they make good neighbors? Isn't it
Where there are cows? But here there are no cows.
Before I built a wall I'd ask to know
What I was walling in or walling out,
And to whom I was like to give offence.
Something there is that doesn't love a wall,
That wants it down." I could say "Elves" to him,
But it's not elves exactly, and I'd rather
He said it for himself. I see him there
Bringing a stone grasped firmly by the top
In each hand, like an old-stone savage armed.
He moves in darkness as it seems to me,
Not of woods only and the shade of trees.

He will not go behind his father's saying,
And he likes having thought of it so well
He says again, "Good fences make good neighbors."

THE MAN WITH THE HOE

Written after seeing Millet's world-famous painting

EDWIN MARKHAM

Bowed by the weight of centuries he leans
Upon his hoe and gazes on the ground,
The emptiness of ages in his face,
And on his back the burden of the world.
Who made him dead to rapture and despair,
A thing that grieves not and that never hopes,
Stolid and stunned, a brother to the ox?
Who loosened and let down this brutal jaw?
Whose was the hand that slanted back this brow?
Whose breath blew out the light within this brain?

Is this the Thing the Lord God made and gave
To have dominion over sea and land;
To trace the stars and search the heavens for power;
To feel the passion of Eternity?
Is this the dream He dreamed who shaped the suns
And marked their ways upon the ancient deep?
Down all the caverns of Hell to their last gulf
There is no shape more terrible than this—
More tongued with censure of the world's blind greed—
More filled with signs and portents for the soul—
More packed with danger to the universe.

What gulfs between him and the seraphim!
Slave of the wheel of labor, what to him
Are Plato and the swing of Pleiades?
What the long reaches of the peaks of song,
The rift of dawn, the reddening of the rose?
Through this dread shape the suffering ages look;
Time's tragedy is in that aching stoop;
Through this dread shape humanity betrayed,
Plundered, profaned, and disinherited,
Cries protest to the Judges of the World,
A protest that is also prophecy.

O masters, lords and rulers in all lands,
Is this the handiwork you gave to God,
This monstrous thing distorted and soul-quenched?
How will you ever straighten up this shape;
Touch it again with immortality;
Give back the upward looking and the light;
Rebuild in it the music and the dream;
Make right the immemorial infamies,
Perfidious wrongs, immedicable woes?

O masters, lords and rulers in all lands,
How will the Future reckon with this man?
How answer his brute question in that hour
When whirlwinds of rebellion shake all shores?
How will it be with kingdoms and with kings—
With those who shaped him to the thing he is—
When this dumb Terror shall rise to judge the world,
After the silence of the centuries?

THE THINKER[1]

BERTON BRALEY

Back of the beating hammer
  By which the steel is wrought,
Back of the workshop's clamor
  The seeker may find the Thought,
The Thought that is ever master
  Of iron and steam and steel,
That rises above disaster
  And tramples it under heel!

The drudge may fret and tinker
  Or labor with dusty blows,
But back of him stands the Thinker,
  The clear-eyed man who Knows;
For into each plough or saber,
  Each piece and part and whole,
Must go the Brains of Labor,
  Which gives the work a soul!

Back of the motors humming,
  Back of the belts that sing,
Back of the hammers drumming,
  Back of the cranes that swing,
There is the eye that scans them,
  Watching through stress and strain,
There is the Mind which plans them,
  Back of the brawn, the Brain!

Might of the roaring boiler,
　　Force of the engine's thrust,
Strength of the sweating toiler,
　　Greatly in these we trust.
But back of them stands the Schemer,
　　The Thinker who drives things through;
Back of the Job—the Dreamer
　　Who's making the dream come true!

BROTHERHOOD

Edwin Markham

Of all things beautiful and good,
The kingliest is brotherhood;
For it will bring again to earth
Her long-lost poesy and mirth;
And till it comes these men are slaves,
And travel downward to the dust of graves.

Clear the way, then, clear the way;
Blind creeds and kings have had their day.
Break the dead branches from the path;
Our hope is in the aftermath.
To this event the ages ran:
Make way for brotherhood—make way for man.

THE FACTORIES

MARGARET WIDDEMER

I have shut my little sister in from life and light
  (For a rose, for a ribbon, for a wreath across my hair),
I have made her restless feet still until the night,
  Locked from sweets of summer and from wild spring air;
I who ranged the meadowlands, free from sun to sun,
  Free to sing and pull the buds and watch the far wings fly,
I have bound my little sister till her playing time was done—
  Oh, my little sister, was it I? Was it I?

I have robbed my sister of her day of maidenhood
  (For a robe, for a feather, for a trinket's restless spark),
Shut from Love till dusk shall fall, how shall she know good,
  How shall she go scatheless through the sin-lit dark?
I who could be innocent, I who could be gay,
  I who could have love and mirth before the light went by,
I have put my sister in her mating-time away—
  Sister, my young sister, was it I? Was it I?

I have robbed my sister of the lips against her breast,
  (For a coin, for the weaving of my children's lace and
    lawn),
Feet that pace beside the loom, hands that cannot rest—
  How can she know motherhood, whose strength is gone?
I who took no heed of her, starved and labor-worn,
  I, against whose placid heart my sleepy gold-heads lie,
Round my path they cry to me, little souls unborn—
  God of Life! Creator! It was I! It was I!

THE HOUSE BY THE SIDE OF THE ROAD

Sam Walter Foss

There are hermit souls that live withdrawn
    In the place of their self-content;
There are souls like stars, that dwell apart,
    In a fellowless firmament;
There are pioneer souls that blaze their paths
    Where highways never ran,—
But let me live by the side of the road
    And be a friend to man.

Let me live in a house by the side of the road
    Where the race of men go by—
The men who are good and the men who are bad,
    As good and as bad as I.
I would not sit in the scorner's seat
    Or hurl the cynic's ban—
Let me live in a house by the side of the road
    And be a friend to man.

I see from my house by the side of the road,
    By the side of the highway of life,
The men who press with the ardor of hope,
    The men who are faint with the strife,
But I turn not away from their smiles and their tears,
    Both parts of an infinite plan—
Let me live in a house by the side of the road
    And be a friend to man.

I know there are brook-gladdened meadows ahead,
    And mountains of wearisome height;

That the road passes on through the long afternoon
   And stretches away to the night.
And still I rejoice when the travellers rejoice
   And weep with the strangers that moan,
Nor live in my house by the side of the road
   Like a man who dwells alone.

Let me live in my house by the side of the road,
   Where the race of men go by—
They are good, they are bad, they are weak, they are
     strong,
   Wise, foolish—so am I.
Then why should I sit in the scorner's seat,
   Or hurl the cynic's ban?
Let me live in my house by the side of the road
   And be a friend to man.

"SCUM O' THE EARTH"

Robert Haven Schauffler

I

At the gate of the West I stand,
On the isle where the nations throng.
We call them "scum o' the earth";

Stay, are we doing you wrong,
Young fellow from Socrates' land?
You, like a Hermes so lissome and strong
Fresh from the Master Praxiteles' hands?
So you're of Spartan birth?
Descended, perhaps, from one of the band—
Deathless in story and song—

Who combed their long hair at Thermopylae's pass?
Ah, I forget the straits, alas!
More tragic than theirs, more compassion-worth
That have doomed you to march in our "immigrant class"
Where you're nothing but "scum o' the earth."

II

You Pole with the child on your knee,
What dower bring you to the land of the free?
Hark! does she croon
That sad little tune
That Chopin once found on his Polish lea
And mounted in gold for you and for me?
Now a ragged young fiddler answers
In wild Czech melody
That Dvorák took whole from the dancers.
And the heavy faces bloom
In the wonderful Slavic way;
The little, dull eyes, the brows a-gloom,
Suddenly dawn like the day,
While, watching these folk and their mystery,
I forget that they're nothing worth;
That Bohemians, Slovaks, Croatians,
And men of all Slavic nations
Are "Polacks":—and "scum o' the earth."

III

Genoese boy of the level brow,
Lad of the lustrous, dreamy eyes
A-stare at Manhattan's pinnacles now
In the first sweet shock of a hushed surprise;
Within your far-rapt seer's eyes
I catch the glow of the wild surmise

That played on the Santa Maria's prow
In that still gray dawn,
Four centuries gone,
When a world from the wave began to rise.
Oh, it's hard to foretell what high emprise
Is the goal that gleams
When Italy's dreams
Spread wing and sweep into the skies.
Caesar dreamed him a world ruled well;
Dante dreamed Heaven out of Hell;
Angelo brought us there to dwell;
And you, are you of a different birth?—
You're only a "dago,"—and "scum o' the earth."

IV

Stay, are we doing you wrong
Calling you "scum o' the earth,"
Man of the sorrow-bowed head,
Of the features tender yet strong,—
Man of the eyes full of wisdom and mystery
Mingled with patience and dread?
Have not I known you in history,
Sorrow-bowed head?
Were you the poet-king, worth
Treasures of Ophir unpriced?
Were you the prophet, perchance, whose art
Foretold how the rabble would mock
That shepherd of spirits, erelong,
Who should carry the lambs on his heart
And tenderly feed his flock?
Man—lift that sorrow-bowed head.
Lo! 'tis the face of the Christ!

The vision dies at its birth.
You're merely a butt for our mirth.
You're a "sheeny"—and therefore despised
And rejected as "scum o' the earth."

V

Countrymen, bend and invoke
Mercy for us blasphemers,
For that we spat on these marvelous folk,
Nations of darers and dreamers,
Scions of singers and seers
Our peers, and more than our peers.
"Rabble and refuse," we name them
And "scum o' the earth," to shame them.
Mercy for us of the few, young years,
Of the culture so callow and crude,
Of the hands so grasping and rude,
The lips so ready for sneers
At the sons of our ancient more-than-peers.
Mercy for us who dare despise
Men in whose loins our Homer lies;
Mothers of men who shall bring to us
The glory of Titian, the grandeur of Huss;
Children in whose frail arms shall rest
Prophets and singers and saints of the West.

Newcomers all from the Eastern seas,
Help us incarnate dreams like these.
Forget, and forgive, that we did you wrong.
Help us to father a nation, strong
In the comradeship of an equal birth,
In the wealth of the richest bloods of earth,

BEAUTY AND TRUTH IN THE COMMONPLACE

"SOME ONE IS COMING TO CALL" (PAGE 142)

THE HAPPIEST HEART

JOHN VANCE CHENEY

Who drives the horses of the sun
　　Shall lord it but a day;
Better the lowly deed were done,
　　And kept the humble way.

The rust shall find the sword of fame,
　　The dust will hide the crown;
Ay, none shall nail so high his name
　　Time will not tear it down.

The happiest heart that ever beat
　　Was in some quiet breast
That found the common daylight sweet,
　　And left to Heaven the rest.

A CONSECRATION[1]

JOHN MASEFIELD

Not of the princes and prelates with periwigged charioteers
Riding triumphantly laurelled to lap the fat of the years,—
Rather the scorned—the rejected—the men hemmed in
　　with the spears;

---

[1] Reprinted from John Masefield's "Salt-Water Ballads." By special
arrangement with The Macmillan Company, Publishers.

The men of the tattered battalion which fights till it dies,
Dazed with the dust of the battle, the din and the cries,
The men with broken heads and the blood running into their
     eyes.

Not the be-medalled Commander, beloved of the throne,
Riding cock-horse to parade when the bugles are blown,
But the lads who carried the koppie and cannot be known.

Not the ruler for me, but the ranker, the tramp of the road,
The slave with the sack on his shoulders pricked on with the
     goad,
The man with too weighty a burden, too weary a load.

The sailor, the stoker of steamers, the man with the clout,
The chantyman bent at the halliards putting a tune to the
     shout,
The drowsy man at the wheel and the tired lookout.

Others may sing of the wine and the wealth and the mirth,
The portly presence of potentates goodly in girth;—
Mine be the dirt and the dross, the dust and scum of the
     earth!

Theirs be the music, the colour, the glory, the gold;
Mine be a handful of ashes, a mouthful of mould.
Of the maimed, of the halt and the blind in the rain and the
     cold—
Of these shall my songs be fashioned, my tales be told.

THE ICE–CART[1]

WILFRID WILSON GIBSON

Perched on my city office-stool,
I watched with envy, while a cool
And lucky carter handled ice. . . .
And I was wandering in a trice,
Far from the grey and grimy heat
Of that intolerable street,
O'er sapphire berg and emerald floe,
Beneath the still, cold ruby glow
Of everlasting Polar night,
Bewildered by the queer half-light,
Until I stumbled, unawares,
Upon a creek where big white bears
Plunged headlong down with flourished heels,
And floundered after shining seals
Through shivering seas of blinding blue.
And as I watched them, ere I knew,
I'd stripped, and I was swimming, too,
Among the seal-pack, young and hale,
And thrusting on with threshing tail,
With twist and twirl and sudden leap
Through crackling ice and salty deep—
Diving and doubling with my kind,
Until at last, we left behind
Those big white, blundering bulks of death,
And lay, at length, with panting breath
Upon a far untraveled floe,
Beneath a gentle drift of snow—

[1] Reprinted from Wilfrid Wilson Gibson's "Collected Poems." By special arrangement with The Macmillan Company, Publishers.

Snow drifting gently, fine and white,
Out of the endless Polar night,
Falling and falling evermore
Upon that far untraveled shore,
Till I was buried fathoms deep
Beneath that cold, white drifting sleep—
Sleep drifting deep,
Deep drifting sleep. . . .

The carter cracked a sudden whip:
I clutched my stool with startled grip,
Awakening to the grimy heat
Of that intolerable street.

SONG

DANA BURNET

Love's on the highroad,
Love's in the byroad—
  Love's on the meadow, and Love's in the mart!
And down every byway
Where I've taken my way
  I've met Love a-smiling—for Love's in my heart!

A BALLADE–CATALOGUE OF LOVELY THINGS

RICHARD LE GALLIENNE

I would make a list against the evil days
  Of lovely things to hold in memory:
First, I would set down my lady's lovely face,
  For earth has no such lovely thing as she;

And next I add, to bear her company,
The great-eyed virgin star that morning brings;
    Then the wild-rose upon its little tree—
So runs my catalogue of lovely things.

The enchanted dogwood, with its ivory trays,
    The water-lily in its sanctuary
Of reeded pools, and dew-drenched lilac sprays,
    For these, of all fair flowers, the fairest be;
    Next write I down the great name of the sea,
Lonely in greatness as the names of kings;
    Then the young moon that hath us all in fee—
So runs my catalogue of lovely things.

Imperial sunsets that in crimson blaze
    Along the hills, and, fairer still to me,
The fireflies dancing in a netted maze
    Woven of twilight and tranquillity;
    Shakespeare and Virgil, their high poesy;
Then a great ship, splendid with snowy wings,
    Voyaging on into eternity—
So runs my catalogue of lovely things.

ENVOI

Prince, not the gold bars of thy treasury,
    Not all thy jewelled sceptres, crowns and rings,
Are worth the honeycomb of the wild bee—
    So runs my catalogue of lovely things.

THE SHEPHERD TO THE POET

Agnes Kendrick Gray

Och, what's the good o' spinnin' words
    As fine as silken thread?
Will "golden gorse upon the hill"
    Be gold to buy ye bread?

An' while ye're list'nin' in the glen
    "To catch the thrush's lay,"
Your thatch is scattered be th' wind,
    Your sheep have gone astray.

Th' time ye're afther makin' rhymes
    O' "leppin' waves an' sea,"
Arrah! ye should be sellin' then
    Your lambs upon the quay.

Sure, 'tis God's ways is very quare,
    An' far beyont my ken,
How o' the selfsame clay he makes
    Poets an' useful men!

THE COMMON STREET

Helen Gray Cone

The common street climbed up against the sky,
    Gray meeting gray; and wearily to and fro
    I saw the patient common people go,
. Each, with his sordid burden, trudging by.

And the rain dropped; there was not any sigh
  Or stir of a live wind; dull, dull and slow
  All motion; as a tale told long ago
The faded world; and creeping night drew nigh.

Then burst the sunset, flooding far and fleet,
  Leavening the whole of life with magic leaven.
    Suddenly down the long wet glistening hill
Pure splendor poured—and lo! the common street,
  A golden highway into golden heaven,
    With the dark shapes of men ascending still.

A STREET CAR MIRACLE

Minnie Leona Upton

The baby laughed—and through the car
  Of dull-eyed folk, at the nightfall weary,
The little silver ripple ran,
And in its wake the smiles began,
  Like sunshine over waters dreary.

The baby laughed—and shoulders bent
  'Neath weight of toil and trouble tragic
Straightened, with motion swift and strong,
As if that burden, carried long,
  Had lifted been by merry magic!

The baby laughed—and one who came
  As slumber stilled that music's ringing,
Looked wondering down the crowded car,
"How brave, how kind, these faces are!"
  He thought, with hope and faith upspringing.

ROSES IN THE SUBWAY

Dana Burnet

A wan-cheeked girl with faded eyes
    Came stumbling down the crowded car,
Clutching her burden to her breast
    As though she held a star.

Roses, I swear it! Red and sweet
    And struggling from her pinched white hands,
Roses . . . like captured hostages
    From far and fairy lands!

The thunder of the rushing train
    Was like a hush . . . The flower scent
Breathed faintly on the stale, whirled air
    Like some dim sacrament—

I saw a garden stretching out
    And morning on it like a crown—
And o'er a bed of crimson bloom
    My mother . . . stooping down.

A TOWN WINDOW

John Drinkwater

Beyond my window in the night
    Is but a drab inglorious street,
Yet there the frost and clean starlight
    As over Warwick woods are sweet.

Under the grey drift of the town
　　The crocus works among the mould
As eagerly as those that crown
　　The Warwick spring in flame and gold.

And when the tramway down the hill
　　Across the cobbles moans and rings,
There is above my window-sill
　　The tumult of a thousand wings.

AN OLD SONG

THOMAS S. JONES, JR.

Low blowing winds from out a midnight sky,
　　The falling embers and a kettle's croon—
These three, but oh, what sweeter lullaby
　　Ever awoke beneath the winter's moon.

We know of none the sweeter, you and I,
　　And oft we've heard together that old tune—
Low blowing winds from out a midnight sky,
　　The falling embers and a kettle's croon.

SMELLS[1]

CHRISTOPHER MORLEY

　　Why is it that the poets tell
　　So little of the sense of smell?
　　These are the odors I love well:

[1] From "The Rocking Horse," by Christopher Morley. Copyright, 1919, by George H. Doran Company, Publishers.

The smell of coffee freshly ground;
Or rich plum pudding, holly crowned;
Or onions fried and deeply browned.

The fragrance of a fumy pipe;
The smell of apples, newly ripe;
And printers' ink on leaden type.

Woods by moonlight in September
Breathe most sweet; and I remember
Many a smoky camp-fire ember.

Camphor, turpentine, and tea,
The balsam of a Christmas tree,
These are whiffs of gramarye. . . .
A ship smells best of all to me!

AFTERNOON

Fannie Stearns Davis Gifford

Some one is coming to call.

Up the red brick path between daffodils dancing
I see white ruffles that blow:
A parasol, dipping against the sun.
It is some one stout, and warm in her new white gloves.

My old green apron is smudged with the garden-mould.
My hands are the hands of a peasant woman. My hair
Comes tumbling down into my eyes.

I wish I could lie down flat like a child
And hide in the grass, while she rings and rings,
And sticks her card under the door with a sigh,
And puffs away down the path.
I wish—but the parasol bobs,
And she bobs like a mandarin's lady,
Smiling and bridling and beckoning.

If I were a daffodil, in an apron of green and gold—

But there she stands on the path,
And her gloves are so new they squeak with newness and
    stoutness.
And I know she will talk of the weather and stay an hour—

If I were a daffodil—
Or a little cool blinking bug
Down in the daffodil leaves—

A CRICKET SINGING IN THE MARKET-PLACE

Louella C. Poole

Down in the city's market-place,
    Today, as I passed by,
Above the tumult and the din
    I heard a cricket cry.
Poor little straying vagabond,
    Wee singer of the street,
Trilling in that mad wilderness
    His song so blithely sweet!

I halted in that busy mart,
  Amongst the produce there,
For suddenly I seemed to see
  A vista wondrous fair—
Of God's great open country,
  Horizons dim and far,
And that same call at even-fall,
  When rose the first pale star.

I saw a brooklet edged with ferns,
  Where tiny minnows play,
Above the glittering golden sands,
  At hide-and-seek all day;
And rustling cornfields, meadows brown,
  A-spangled with the dew;
The hills with Indian summer haze
  Ethereal and blue.

I heard the tinkling cow-bells,
  And smelt the breath of kine,
The scent of ripening orchards,
  Grapes purpling on the vine.
O vision fair revealing
  Such range of time and space!
Moved nigh to tears, in softened mood
  I left the market-place.

Ah, minstrel gay, wee troubadour
  With voice so shrilly sweet,
You little knew what power you had
  To spur my lagging feet,

And bear my spirit far away
 From all that rush and roar,
To God's own blessed country
 And happy days of yore!

THE MONKEY

NANCY CAMPBELL

I saw you hunched and shivering on the stones,
The bleak wind piercing to your fragile bones,
Your shabby scarlet all inadequate:
A little ape that had such human eyes
They seemed to hide behind their miseries—
Their dumb and hopeless bowing down to fate—
Some puzzled wonder. Was your monkey soul
Sickening with memories of gorgeous days,
Of tropic playfellows and forest ways,
Where, agile, you could swing from bole to bole
In an enchanted twilight with great flowers
For stars; or on a bough the long night hours
Sit out in rows, and chatter at the moon?
Shuffling you went, your tiny chilly hand
Outstretched for what you did not understand;
Your puckered mournful face begging a boon
That but enslaved you more. They who passed by
Saw nothing sorrowful; gave laugh or stare,
Unheeding that the little antic there
Played in the gutter such a tragedy.

IN SERVICE

Winifred M. Letts

Little Nellie Cassidy has got a place in town,
  She wears a fine white apron,
  She wears a new black gown,
An' the quarest little cap at all with straymers hanging down.

I met her one fine evening stravagin' down the street,
  A feathered hat upon her head,
  And boots upon her feet.
"Och, Mick," says she, "may God be praised that you and I
  should meet.

"It's lonesome in the city with such a crowd," says she;
  "I'm lost without the bog-land,
  I'm lost without the sea,
An' the harbor an' the fishing-boats that sail out fine and free.

"I'd give a golden guinea to stand upon the shore,
  To see the big waves lepping,
  To hear them splash and roar,
To smell the tar and the drying nets, I'd not be asking more.

"To see the small white houses, their faces to the sea,
  The childher in the doorway,
  Or round my mother's knee;
For I'm strange and lonesome missing them, God keep them
  all," says she.

Little Nellie Cassidy earns fourteen pounds and more,
  Waiting on the quality,
  And answering the door—
But her heart is some place far away upon the Wexford shore.

TO A PHOTOGRAPHER[1]

BERTON BRALEY

I have known love and woe and toil and fight;
  I have lived largely, I have dreamed and planned,
  And Time, the Sculptor, with a master-hand
Has graven on my face for all men's sight
Deep lines of joy and sorrow, growth and blight,
  Of labor and of service and command
  —And now you show me this,—this waxen, bland,
And placid face,—unlined, unwrinkled, white!

This is not I—this fatuous thing you show,
  Retouched and smoothed and prettified to please;
Put back the wrinkles and the lines I know;
  I have spent blood and brain achieving these.
Out of the pain, the struggle and the wrack,
These are my scars of battle—put them back!

A SAINT'S HOURS

SARAH NORCLIFFE CLEGHORN

HER MATINS

In the still cold before the sun,
  Her brothers and her sisters small
She woke, and washed and dressed each one.

[1] From "Songs of the Workaday World," by Berton Braley. Copyright, 1915, by George H. Doran Company, Publishers.

PRIME

And through the morning hours all
  Singing above her broom she stood
And swept the house from hall to hall.

TIERCE

Then out she ran with tidings good,
  Across the fields and down the lane,
To share them with the neighborhood.

SEXT

Four miles she walked, and home again,
  To sit through half the afternoon
To hear a feeble crone complain.

NONES

But when she saw the frosty moon
  And lakes of shadow on the hill,
Her maiden dreams grew bright as noon.

VESPERS

She threw her pitying apron frill
  Over a little trembling mouse
When the sleek cat yawned on the sill.

EVENSONG

In the late hours and drowsy house
  At last, too tired, beside her bed
She fell asleep—her prayers half said.

THE MOVIES

FLORENCE KIPER FRANK

She knows a cheap release
    From worry and from pain—
The cowboys spur their horses
    Over the unending plain.

The tenement walls are small;
    Their walls press on the brain.
Oh, the dip of the galloping horses
    On the limitless, wind-swept plain!

THE FARMER OF WESTERHA'

JAMES LOGIE ROBERTSON

Abune the braes I see him stand,
The tapmost corner o' his land,
An' scan wi' care, owre hill an' plain,
A prospect he may ca' his ain.

His yowes ayont the hillocks feed,
Weel herdit in by wakefu' Tweed;
An' canny thro' the bent his kye
Gang creepin' to the byre doun-by.

His hayfields lie fu' smoothly shorn,
An' ripenin' rise his rigs o' corn;
A simmer's evenin' glory fa's
Upon his hamestead's sober wa's.

A stately figure there he stands
An' rests upon his staff his hands:
Maist like some patriarch of eld,
In sic an evenin' calm beheld.

A farmer he of Ochilside,
For worth respectit far an' wide;
A friend of justice and of truth,
A favorite wi' age and youth.

There's no' a bairn but kens him weel,
And ilka collie's at his heel;
Nor beast nor body e'er had ocht
To wyte him wi', in deed or thoucht.

Fu' mony a gloamin' may he stand
Abune the brae to bless the land!
Fu' mony a simmer rise an' fa'
In beauty owre his couthie ha'!

For peacefu' aye, as simmer's air,
The kindly hearts that kindle there;
Whase friendship, sure an' aye the same,
For me mak's Ochilside a hame.

The Ochil Hills are between Forth and Tay, in southwestern Perthshire; so *Tweed* must be the name of the farmer's collie.

abune the braes: above the hillsides; *ca' his ain:* call his own; *yowes:* ewes; *canny thro' the bent:* quietly through the grassy hillocks; *kye:* cows; *doun-by:* close at hand; *fu':* full; *sic:* such; *ilka:* each; *wyte:* blame; *couthie:* comfortable.

THE GREAT LOVER

RUPERT BROOKE

I have been so great a lover: filled my days
So proudly with the splendor of Love's praise,
The pain, the calm, and the astonishment,
Desire illimitable, and still content,
And all dear names men use, to cheat despair,
For the perplexed and viewless streams that bear
Our hearts at random down the dark of life.
Now, ere the unthinking silence on that strife
Steals down, I would cheat drowsy Death so far,
My night shall be remembered for a star
That outshone all the suns of all men's days.
Shall I not crown them with immortal praise
Whom I have loved, who have given me, dared with me
High secrets, and in darkness knelt to see
The inenarrable[1] godhead of delight?
Love is a flame:—we have beaconed the world's night.
A city:—and we have built it, these and I.
An emperor:—we have taught the world to die.
So, for their sakes I loved, ere I go hence,
And for the high cause of Love's magnificence,
And to keep loyalties young, I'll write those names
Golden for ever, eagles, crying flames,
And set them as a banner, that men may know,
To dare the generations, burn, and blow
Out on the wind of Time, shining and streaming. . . .
These I have loved:

            White plates and cups, clean-gleaming,
Ringed with blue lines; and feathery, faery dust;

[1] *inenarrable:* unspeakable; indescribable.

Wet roofs, beneath the lamp-light; the strong crust
Of friendly bread; and many-tasting food;
Rainbows; and the blue bitter smoke of wood;
And radiant raindrops couching in cool flowers;
And flowers themselves, that sway through sunny hours,
Dreaming of moths that drink them under the moon;
Then, the cool kindliness of sheets, that soon
Smooth away trouble; and the rough male kiss
Of blankets; grainy wood; live hair that is
Shining and free; blue-massing clouds; the keen
Unpassioned beauty of a great machine;
The benison of hot water; furs to touch;
The good smell of old clothes; and other such—
The comfortable smell of friendly fingers,
Hair's fragrance, and the musty reek that lingers
About dead leaves and last year's ferns. . . .

                       Dear names,
And thousand others throng to me! Royal flames;
Sweet water's dimpling laugh from tap or spring;
Holes in the ground; and voices that do sing;
Voices in laughter, too; and body's pain,
Soon turned to peace; and the deep-panting train;
Firm sands; the little dulling edge of foam
That browns and dwindles as the wave goes home;
And washen stones, gay for an hour; the cold
Graveness of iron; moist black earthen mold;
Sleep; and high places; footprints in the dew;
And oaks; and brown horse-chestnuts, glossy-new;
And new-peeled sticks; and shining pools on grass;—
All these have been my loves. And these shall pass.
Whatever passes not, in the great hour,
Nor all my passion, all my prayers, have power
To hold them with me through the gate of Death.

They'll play deserter, turn with the traitor breath,
Break the high bond we made, and sell Love's trust
And sacramented covenant to the dust.
—Oh, never a doubt but, somewhere, I shall wake,
And give what's left of love again, and make
New friends, now strangers. . . .
                But the best I've known,
Stays here, and changes, breaks, grows old, is blown
About the winds of the world, and fades from brains
Of living men, and dies.
                Nothing remains.
O dear my loves, O faithless, once again
This one last gift I give: that after men
Shall know, and later lovers, far-removed,
Praise you, "All these were lovely"; say, "He loved."

"WHAT RICHES HAVE YOU"

George Santayana

What riches have you that you deem me poor,
    Or what large comfort that you call me sad?
    Tell me what makes you so exceeding glad:
Is your earth happy, or your heaven sure?
I hope for heaven, since the stars endure
    And bring such tidings as our fathers had.
    I know no deeper doubt to make me mad,
I need no brighter love to keep me pure.
To me the faiths of old are daily bread;
    I bless their hope, I bless their will to save,
And my deep heart still meaneth what they said.
    It makes me happy that the soul is brave,
And, being so much kinsman to the dead,
    I walk contented to the peopled grave.

PLACES AND PERSONS

"ALL ACROSS THE GLADES OF FERN HE CALLS HIS
MERRY MEN" (PAGE 179)

NAMES

ABBIE FARWELL BROWN

From Somerset and Devon,
    From Kent and Lincolnshire,
The younger sons came sailing
    With hearts of steel and fire.

From leafy lane and valley,
    From glebe and ancient wood,
The counties of old England
    Poured forth their warmest blood.

Out of the gray-walled cities,
    Away from the castled towns,
Corners of thatch and roses,
    Heathery combes and downs,

With neither crown nor penny,
    But an iron will they came,
Heirs of an old tradition
    And a good old English name.

A brooding silence met them
    On a nameless, savage shore;
But they called the wild—"New England,"
    For the sake of the blood they bore.

"Plymouth, Exeter, Bristol,
Boston, Windsor, Wells."
Beloved names of England
  Rang in their hearts like bells.

They named their rocky farmlands,
  Their hamlets by the sea,
For the mother-towns that bred them
  In racial loyalty.

"Cambridge, Hartford, Gloucester,
Hampton, Norwich, Stowe."
The younger sons looked backward
  And sealed their sonship so.

The old blood thrills in answer,
  As centuries go by,
To names that meant a challenge,
  A signal, or a sigh.

Now over friendly waters
  The old towns, each to each,
Call with the kinship in a name;
  One race, one truth, one speech.

ACROSS ILLINOIS

John Stoltze

The feel of the friendly prairies, the softening shadows of
    night
That covers the flattened landscape to the distant gleam of a
    light.

The even swing of the trainload over the singing rails
Between the flowing fences that border the straight steel
    trails.

The light of a locomotive adown the level track,
A straight white line of brightness cutting the blanket of
    black.

The roar of the whistling steam, a flickering lighted train;
Once more the soft black silence and the hum of the rails
    again.

And through it all the darkness, keener than sense or sight,
The feel of the friendly prairies, the shadow of Western
    night.

ON THE PALISADES

Louis Untermeyer

And still we climbed,
Upward into those sheer and threatening cliffs
Storming against the sky.
As though to stop our impudent assault,
The sun laid great hot hands upon our backs,
And bent them down.
There were no bluff, good-humored winds to push us on;
There were no shrubs to grasp, no staff to aid:
Laughter was all we leaned on.

We dared not turn to view the dizzy depth; and then
At last the height, and the long climb over!
And laughing still, we drew long, panting breaths;

And our pulses jumped with a proud and foolish thrill,
As though we had gained not merely the top of a hill,
But a victory.

Up here the gaunt earth seemed to sprawl,
Stretching its legs beyond the cramping skies,
And lie upon its cloudy back and yawn.
Rhythmical breezes arose,
Like a strong man awaking from sleep,
Like the measured breathing of Day.
And the earth stirred and called us.
An unseen path sprang from the undergrowth,
And dodged among the bushes lightly, beckoning us on;
Vine-snares and rocks made way for us;
Daisies threw themselves before our feet;
The eager little armies of the grass,
Waving their happy spears, ran on beside us:
And when we slackened, when we thought of resting,
The running grasses stopped, the earth sank back into itself,
Became a living pillow, a soft breast,
And every branch held out its comforting arms.
The winds pressed close, and, growing gentle, sang to us;
And so we sat beneath the mothering trees.

Languor leaned down
And, whispering peace, drew us into ourselves;
And in the drowsy sunlight
We mused, escaping from the clanging world,
Happy to sink in visions and soft fantasies
For solace and for strength;
To dip into a dream, as into sleep,
And wring new ardor from it, and rise refreshed;
Irradiant, held by no soothing past,
Blundering brightly on.

Then, in an unseen flash,
The air was sharp with energy again;
The afternoon tingled and snapped, electric with laughter.
And he, our friend and lover, our buoyant, swaggering boy,—
His soul as fiery as his flaming hair,—
Began to sing this snatch of ancient rhyme
Caught from the pickers in the cotton-fields:

> *"Lord He thought He'd make a man,*
> *(Dese bones gwine ter rise again.)*
> *Made him out er earth an' a han'ful er san'.*
> *(Dese bones gwine ter rise again.)*

> *"I know it; indeed, I know it, brudders;*
> *I know it. Dese bones gwine ter rise again.*

> *"Thought He'd make an 'umman, too;*
> *Didn't know 'zackly what ter do.*
> *(Dese bones gwine ter rise again.)*

> *"Tuk one rib f'om Adam's side.*
> *Made Miss Eve for to be his bride.*
> *(Dese bones gwine ter rise again.)"*

Five hundred feet below us lay the world.
The Sunday-colored crowds busy at play,
The children, the tawdry lovers, and the far-off tremor of
    ships,
Came to us, caught us out of the blurring vastness,
As things remembered from dreams.
And still he sang, while we joined in with childlike eagerness
The deep infectious music of a childlike race:

"*Sot 'em in a gyarden rich an' fair;*
  Tol' 'em dey could eat w'atever wuz dere,
    (*Dese bones gwine ter rise again.*)

"*F'om one tree you mus' not eat;*
  Ef you do, you'll have to skeet!
    (*Dese bones gwine ter rise again.*)

"*Sarpint woun' him roun' er trunk;*
  At Miss Eve his eye he wunk.
    (*Dese bones gwine ter rise again.*)

"*I know it; indeed, I know it, brudders;*
  I know it—"

Like a blue snake uncoiled,
The lazy river, stretching between the banks,
Smoothed out its rippling folds, splotchy with sunlight,
And slept again, basking in silence.
A sea-gull chattered stridently;
We heard, breaking the rhythms of the song,
The cough of the asthmatic motor-boat
Spluttering toward the pier.
And stillness again.

"*Lord He come wid a 'ponstrous voice;*
  Shook dis whole earth to its joists.
    (*Dese bones gwine ter rise again.*)

"'*Adam, Adam, where art thou?*'
  '*Yas, good Lord, I's a-comin' now.*'
    (*Dese bones gwine ter rise again.*)

"'*Stole my apples, I believe—*'
  '*No, Marse Lord, I 'speck 'twas Eve.*'
    (*Dese bones gwine ter rise again.*)"

The little boat drew nearer toward the land,
Still puffing like a wheezy runner out of breath.
And we could see, crowding its narrow decks,
The little human midges, remote and so unhuman,
Seeming to belong less to life than the fearless ants,
That swarmed upon the remnants of our lunch,
Heedless of all the gods on whom they casually dared to
    climb.
So far the people seemed!
And still a faint stirring reached us;
A thin thread of music flung its airy filaments toward heaven,
Where we, the happy deities, sat enthroned.
Straining our ears, we caught the slender tone,
"*Darling, I am growing old; silver threads among—*"
And then it broke,
And over us rushed the warm flood of the human need.
Out of the frayed, cheap song something thrust out
And gripped us like a warm and powerful hand.
No longer Olympian, aloof upon our solemn eminence,
We crumbled on our heights and yearned to them.
The very distance had a chill for us.
What if, of a sudden, the boat should topple and plunge;
And there should rise a confused cry of people, and the faint,
    high voice of a child;
And heads should bob in the water, and sink like rotten
    corks,
And we, up here so helpless,
Unhuman, and remote—

A twilight mist stole up the bay;
In a near-by clump a screech-owl wailed;
A breeze blew strangely cold, and, with a covert haste,
We gathered up our things, whistled a breath too loud,

And took the path down to the earth we knew—
The earth we knew, the dear and casual world
Of sleep that followed struggle, struggle that called from
　　　sleep—
The harsh, beloved, immortal invitation.

And as we walked the song sprang up again;
And as we sang the words took on new power and majesty.
The dying sun became a part of them,
Gathering his fires in one last singing beam,
In one bright, lyric death.
The skies caught up the chorus, thundering it back
From every cranny of the windy heavens;
And, rising from the rocks and silent waters,
Hailing the happy energy as its own,
The flood of life laughed with that gay conviction:
I know it. Indeed, I know it, brothers,
I know it. These bones will rise again.
Lulled by no soft and easy dreams,
Out of the crowded agonies of birth on birth,
Refreshed and radiant,
These bones will rise.
Out of the very arms of cradling Death,
These bones!

ST. MAIXENT

The Cathedral: Early Morning

ALLEN CRAFTON

The stern gray glory of old days is still
Upon it! Like old ghosts the dawn mists fill
Its hollows, hovering in the moveless air.
A bent old woman nears its wide-arched door,

Her sabots tapping the worn flags before
Its pallid, patterned walls.
Her hooded face recalls
A tall white candle lighted long ago,
Now in its blackened sconce burned low.

Sudden the shameless conquering sun
Sweeps from the spires the centuries;
And there uprears a crumbling pile of stone;
Bleak, ugly, set athwart the ways
Of unsouled latter days.
He wakens life: with a long rasping sound
A maid swings back the shutters;
Wooden sabots clatter up the streets;
A bicyclist rides by; a madam greets
Her crone before the wide-arched door and utters
In a shrill voice the latest cinema news. . . .

THE KING'S HIGHWAY

"*El Camino Real*"

JOHN STEVEN MCGROARTY

All in the golden weather, forth let us ride to-day,
You and I together, on the King's Highway,
The blue skies above us, and below the shining sea;
There's many a road to travel, but it's this road for me.

It's a long road and sunny, and the fairest in the world—
There are peaks that rise above it in their snowy mantles
    curled,
And it leads from the mountains through a hedge of
    chaparral,
Down to the waters where the sea gulls call.

It's a long road and sunny, it's a long road and old,
And the brown padres made it for the flocks of the fold;
They made it for the sandals of the sinner-folk that trod
From the fields in the open to the shelter-house of God.

They made it for the sandals of the sinner-folk of old;
Now the flocks they are scattered and death keeps the fold;
But you and I together we will take the road to-day,
With the breath in our nostrils, on the King's Highway.

We will take the road together through the morning's golden
    glow,
And we'll dream of those who trod it in the mellowed long
    ago;
We will stop at the Missions where the sleeping padres lay,
And we'll bend a knee above them for their souls' sake to
    pray.

We'll ride through the valleys where the blossom's on the
    tree,
Through the orchards and the meadows with the bird and
    the bee,
And we'll take the rising hills where the manzanitas grow,
Past the gray tails of waterfalls where blue violets blow.

Old Conquistadores, O brown priests and all,
Give us your ghosts for company when night begins to fall;
There's many a road to travel, but it's this road to-day,
With the breath of God about us on the King's Highway.

THE BOSTON SYMPHONY ORCHESTRA

JAMES FENIMORE COOPER, Jr.

Dark-coated men with instruments: a sound,
  Tentative, groping—as each seeks to pitch
  This string to that—this key—one knows not which,
Each questioning note by other questions drowned.
The blundering horns, with shining mouths and round,
  The 'cellos quivering their contralto rich,
  The pastoral flutes, whose crystal notes bewitch,
Expectant all—till some accord be found.
The leader lifts his slender rod, and lo,
  The turmoil dies—and as we strain to hear
    With one quick sweep the miracle is done—
    A myriad wandering notes are bound in one—
  One many-throated voice, impassioned, clear,
Instinct with things we seek but cannot know.

MEN OF HARLAN

WILLIAM ASPENWALL BRADLEY

Here in the level country, where the creeks run straight and
  wide,
Six men upon their pacing nags may travel side by side,
But the mountain men of Harlan, you may tell them all the
  while,
When they pass through our village, for they ride in single
  file.
And the children, when they see them, stop their play and
  stand and cry:
"Here come the men of Harlan, men of Harlan, riding by."

O the mountain men of Harlan, when they come down to the
   plain,
With dangling stirrup, jangling spur, and loosely hanging rein,
They do not ride, like our folks here, in twos and threes
   abreast,
With merry laughter, talk and song, and lightly spoken jest;
But silently and solemnly, in long and straggling line,
As you may see them in the hills, beyond Big Black and Pine.

For, in that far strange country, where the men of Harlan
   dwell,
There are no roads at all, like ours, as we've heard travelers
   tell,
But only narrow trails that wind along each shallow creek,
Where the silence hangs so heavy, you can hear the leathers
   squeak.
And there no two can ride abreast, but each alone must go,
Picking his way as best he may, with careful steps and slow,

Down many a shelving ledge of shale, skirting the trembling
   sands,
Through many a pool and many a pass, where the mountain
   laurel stands
So thick and close to left and right, with holly bushes, too,
The clinging branches meet midway to bar the passage
   through,—
O'er many a steep and stony ridge, o'er many a high divide,
And so it is the Harlan men thus one by one do ride.

Yet it is strange to see them pass in line through our wide
   street,
When they come down to sell their sang, and buy their stores
   of meat,

These silent men, in somber black all clad from foot to head,
Though they have left their lonely hills and the narrow
    creek's rough bed.
And 'tis no wonder children stop their play and stand and
    cry:
"Here come the men of Harlan, men of Harlan, riding by."

HARBURY

Louise Driscoll

All the men of Harbury go down to the sea in ships,
The wind upon their faces, the salt upon their lips.

The little boys of Harbury, when they are laid to sleep,
Dream of masts and cabins and the wonders of the deep.

The women-folk of Harbury have eyes like the sea,
Wide with watching wonder, deep with mystery.

I met a woman: "Beyond the bar," she said,
"Beyond the shallow water where the green lines spread,

"Out beyond the sand-bar and the white spray,
My three sons wait for the Judgment Day."

I saw an old man who goes to sea no more,
Watch from morn to evening down on the shore.

"The sea's a hard mistress," the old man said;
"The sea is always hungry and never full fed.

"The sea had my father and took my son from me—
Sometimes I think I see them, walking on the sea!

"I'd like to be in Harbury on the Judgment Day,
When the word is spoken and the sea is wiped away,

"And all the drowned fisher boys with sea-weed in their hair,
Rise and walk to Harbury to meet the women there.

"I'd like to be in Harbury to see the souls arise,
Son and mother hand in hand, lovers with glad eyes.

"I think there would be many who would turn and look with
  me,
Hoping for another glimpse of the cruel sea!

"They tell me that in Paradise the fields are green and still;
With pleasant flowers everywhere that all may take who will,

"And four great rivers flowing from out the throne of God
That no one ever drowns in and souls may cross dry-shod.

"I think among those wonders there will be men like me
Who miss the old salt danger of the singing sea.

"For in my heart, like some old shell, inland, safe, and dry,
Any one who harks will still hear the sea cry."

THE LAKE ISLE OF INNISFREE[1]

William Butler Yeats

I will arise and go now, and go to Innisfree,
  And a small cabin build there, of clay and wattles made;
Nine bean rows will I have there, a hive for the honey bee,
  And live alone in the bee-loud glade.

[1] Reprinted from William Butler Yeats's "Selected Poems." By
special arrangement with The Macmillan Company, Publishers.

And I shall have some peace there, for peace comes dropping
    slow,
  Dropping from the veils of the morning to where the
    cricket sings;
There midnight's all a glimmer, and noon a purple glow,
  And evening full of the linnet's wings.

I will arise and go now, for always night and day,
  I hear lake-water lapping with low sounds by the shore;
While I stand on the roadway, or on the pavements gray,
  I hear it in the deep heart's core.

COTSWOLD LOVE

John Drinkwater

Blue skies are over Cotswold
  And April snows go by,
The lasses turn their ribbons
  For April's in the sky.
And April is the season
  When Sabbath girls are dressed,
From Rodboro' to Campden,
  In all their silken best.

An ankle is a marvel
  When first the buds are brown,
And not a lass but knows it
  From Stow to Gloucester town.
And not a girl goes walking
  Along the Cotswold lanes
But knows men's eyes in April
  Are quicker than their brains.

It's little that it matters,
    So long as you're alive,
If you're eighteen in April,
    Or rising sixty-five,
When April comes to Amberley
    With skies of April blue,
And Cotswold girls are briding
    With slyly tilted shoe.

THE LITTLE WAVES OF BREFFNY

Eva Gore-Booth

The grand road from the mountains goes shining to the sea,
    And there is traffic on it, and many a horse and cart;
But the little roads of Cloonagh are dearer far to me,
    And the little roads of Cloonagh go rambling through my
        heart.

A great storm from the ocean goes shouting o'er the hill,
    And there is glory in it, and terror on the wind;
But the haunted air of twilight is very strange and still,
    And the little winds of twilight are dearer to my mind.

The great waves of the Atlantic sweep storming on their way,
    Shining green and silver with the hidden herring shoal;
But the Little Waves of Breffny have drenched my heart in
    spray,
    And the Little Waves of Breffny go stumbling through my
        soul.

DUNA

MARJORIE L. C. PICKTHALL

When I was a little lad
　　With folly on my lips,
Fain was I for journeying
　　All the seas in ships.
But now across the southern swell,
　　Every dawn I hear
The little streams of Duna
　　Running clear.

When I was a young man,
　　Before my beard was gray,
All to ships and sailormen
　　I gave my heart away.
But I'm weary of the sea-wind,
　　I'm weary of the foam,
And the little stars of Duna
　　Call me home.

"O, FALMOUTH IS A FINE TOWN"

WILLIAM ERNEST HENLEY

O, Falmouth is a fine town with ships in the bay,
And I wish from my heart that it's there I was to-day;
I wish from my heart I was far away from here,
Sitting in my parlor and talking to my dear.
　　For it's home, dearie, home—it's home I want to be.
　　Our topsails are hoisted, and we'll away to sea.
　　O the oak and the ash and the bonny birken tree,
　　They're all growing green in the old countrie!

In Baltimore a-walking a lady I did meet
With her babe on her arm as she came down the street;
And I thought how I sailed, and the cradle standing ready
For the pretty little babe that has never seen its daddie.
    And it's home, dearie, home. . . .

O, if it be a lass, she shall wear a golden ring;
And if it be a lad, he shall fight for his king;
With his dirk and his hat and his little jacket blue
He shall walk the quarter-deck as his daddie used to do.
    And it's home, dearie, home. . . .

O, there's a wind a-blowing, a-blowing from the west,
And that of all the winds is the one I like the best;
For it blows at our backs, and it shakes our pennon free,
And it soon will blow us home to the old countrie.
    For it's home, dearie, home—it's home I want to be.
    Our topsails are hoisted, and we'll away to sea.
    O the oak and the ash and the bonny birken tree,
    They're all growing green in the old countrie!

THE WEST WIND[1]

JOHN MASEFIELD

It's a warm wind, the west wind, full of birds' cries;
I never hear the west wind but tears are in my eyes.
For it comes from the west lands, the old brown hills,
And April's in the west wind, and daffodils.

[1] Reprinted from John Masefield's "Collected Poems." By special arrangement with The Macmillan Company, Publishers.

It's a fine land, the west land, for hearts as tired as mine,
Apple orchards blossom there, and the air's like wine.
There is cool green grass there, where men may lie at rest,
And the thrushes are in song there, fluting from the nest.

"Will you not come home, brother? You have been long
    away.
It's April, and blossom time, and white is the spray;
And bright is the sun, brother, and warm is the rain,—
Will you not come home, brother, home to us again?

The young corn is green, brother, where the rabbits run;
It's blue sky, and white clouds, and warm rain and sun.
It's song to a man's soul, brother, fire to a man's brain,
To hear the wild bees and see the merry spring again.

Larks are singing in the west, brother, above the green wheat,
So will you not come home, brother, and rest your tired
    feet?
I've a balm for bruised hearts, brother, sleep for aching eyes,"
Says the warm wind, the west wind, full of birds' cries.

It's the white road westwards is the road I must tread
To the green grass, the cool grass, and rest for heart and
    head,
To the violets and the brown brooks and the thrushes' song
In the fine land, the west land, the land where I belong.

"AS I CAME DOWN FROM LEBANON"

CLINTON SCOLLARD

As I came down from Lebanon,
Came winding, wandering slowly down
Through mountain-passes bleak and brown,
The cloudless day was well-nigh done.
The city, like an opal, set
In emerald, showed each minaret
Afire with radiant beams of sun.
And glistened orange, fig, and lime
Where song-birds made melodious chime,
As I came down from Lebanon.

As I came down from Lebanon,
Like lava in the dying glow,
Through olive orchards far below
I saw the murmuring river run,
And 'neath the wall upon the sand
Swart sheiks from distant Samarkand
With precious spices they had won,
Lay long and languidly in wait
Till they might pass the guarded gate,
As I came down from Lebanon.

As I came down from Lebanon,
I saw strange men from lands afar
In mosque and square and gay bazaar,
The Magi that the Moslem shun,
The grave Effendi from Stamboul
Who sherbet sipped in corners cool;

And, from the balconies o'errun
With roses, gleamed the eyes of those
Who dwell in still seraglios,
As I came down from Lebanon.

As I came down from Lebanon,
The flaming flower of daytime died,
And Night, arrayed as is a bride
Of some great king, in garments spun
Of purple and the finest gold,
Out-bloomed in glories manifold!
Until the moon above the dun
And darkening desert, void of shade,
Shone like a keen Damascus blade,
As I came down from Lebanon!

ACROSS THE FIELDS TO ANNE

RICHARD BURTON

How often in the summer-tide,
His graver business set aside,
Has stripling Will, the thoughtful-eyed,
    As to the pipe of Pan,
Stepped blithesomely with lover's pride
    Across the fields to Anne.

It must have been a merry mile,
This summer stroll by hedge and stile,
With sweet foreknowledge all the while
    How sure the pathway ran
To dear delights of kiss and smile
    Across the fields to Anne.

The silly sheep that graze to-day,
I wot, they let him go his way,
Nor once looked up, as who should say:
   "It is a seemly man."
For many lads went wooing aye
  Across the fields to Anne.

The oaks, they have a wiser look;
Mayhap they whispered to the brook:
"The world by him shall yet be shook,
  It is in Nature's plan;
Though now he fleets like any rook
  Across the fields to Anne."

And I am sure, that on some hour
Coquetting soft, 'twixt sun and shower,
He stooped and broke a daisy-flower
  With heart of tiny span,
And bore it as a lover's dower
  Across the fields to Anne.

While from her cottage garden-bed
She plucked a jasmine's goodlihede,
To scent his jerkin's brown instead;
  Now since that love began,
What luckier swain than he who sped
  Across the fields to Anne?

The winding path whereon I pace,
The hedgerow's green, the summer's grace,
Are still before me face to face;
  Methinks I almost can
Turn poet and join the singing race
  Across the fields to Anne!

A SONG OF SHERWOOD

ALFRED NOYES

Sherwood in the twilight, is Robin Hood awake?
Gray and ghostly shadows are gliding through the brake,
Shadows of a dappled deer, dreaming of the morn,
Dreaming of a shadowy man that winds a shadowy horn.

Robin Hood is here again: all his merry thieves
Hear a ghostly bugle-note shivering through the leaves,
Calling as he used to call, faint and far away,
In Sherwood, in Sherwood, about the break of day.

Merry, Merry England has kissed the lips of June:
All the wings of fairyland were here beneath the moon,
Like a flight of rose-leaves fluttering in a mist
Of opal and ruby and pearl and amethyst.

Merry, Merry England is waking as of old,
With eyes of blither hazel and hair of brighter gold:
For Robin Hood is here again beneath the bursting spray
In Sherwood, in Sherwood, about the break of day.

Love is in the greenwood building him a house
Of wild rose and hawthorn and honeysuckle boughs:
Love is in the greenwood; dawn is in the skies;
And Marian is waiting with a glory in her eyes.

Hark! The dazzled laverock climbs the golden steep!
Marian is waiting: is Robin Hood asleep?
Round the fairy grass-rings frolic elf and fay,
In Sherwood, in Sherwood, about the break of day.

Oberon, Oberon, rake away the gold,
Rake away the red leaves, roll away the mould,
Rake away the gold leaves, roll away the red,
And wake Will Scarlett from his leafy forest bed.

Friar Tuck and Little John are riding down together
With quarter-staff and drinking-can and gray goose-feather.
The dead are coming back again; the years are rolled away
In Sherwood, in Sherwood, about the break of day.

Softly over Sherwood the south wind blows.
All the heart of England hid in every rose
Hears across the greenwood the sunny whisper leap,
Sherwood in the red dawn, is Robin Hood asleep?

Hark, the voice of England wakes him as of old
And, shattering the silence with a cry of brighter gold,
Bugles in the greenwood echo from the steep,
Sherwood in the red dawn, is Robin Hood asleep?

Where the deer are gliding down the shadowy glen
All across the glades of fern he calls his merry men—
Doublets of the Lincoln green glancing through the May
In Sherwood, in Sherwood, about the break of day—

Calls them and they answer: from aisles of oak and ash
Rings the *Follow! Follow!* and the boughs begin to crash;
The ferns begin to flutter and the flowers begin to fly;
And through the crimson dawning the robber band goes by.

Robin! Robin! Robin! All his merry thieves
Answer as the bugle-note shivers through the leaves,
Calling as he used to call, faint and far away,
In Sherwood, in Sherwood, about the break of day.

THE BARD OF AULD LANG SYNE

James Main Dixon

What tuneful bard of auld lang syne
  Wi' Robbie can compare?
Who sings the home of me and mine,
  The bonnie banks of Ayr;

The daisy with its crimson tips
  That nestles 'mid the dew;
The fragrant rose, with ruddy lips,
  And thorns—if love's untrue;

The laverock springing from its nest
  At the first peep of day,
To wake the shepherd from his rest,
  And singing soar away.

I stand beside the reapers strong
  Among the bearded bear,
I hear the mavis' mellow song
  When eventide is near.

I see auld ruined castles gray
  Nod grimly to the moon,
And Hornie waiting for his prey,
  To fricht with eldritch croon;

And Alloway's auld haunted kirk
  Among the sheeted dead,
Where witches foot it in the mirk
  By supple Nannie led.

The auld clay-biggin's walls appear;
    And ben the hallan there,
From a hushed household group I hear
    The sound of evening prayer.

Hail to the bard who sings the praise
    Of Scots who fought and bled
At Stirling Bridge and Loudon Braes
    With Wallace at their head;

And who at glorious Bannockburn,
    With Bruce the bauld and slee,
Made Edward like a coward turn
    And to the borders flee.

Rab's lines are like the burning gleed,
    They warm us, make us wiser;
But may we better reck the rede
    Than ever did the adviser!

From his wee sleekit mouse I take
    That word with wisdom fraught,
The best constructed plans we make
    Will often come to naught.

From him I get that noble rule—
    The man of upright mind,
Who scorns to palter and to snool,
    Is king among mankind.

Syne: pronounced with sibilant "s" as in "since"; *auld lang syne:* old long ago (since); *bear:* barley; *Hornie:* the devil; *eldritch:* weird; *mirk:* darkness; *ben the hallan:* inside the doorway partition; *bauld and slee:* bold and crafty (sly); *gleed:* red ember; *reck the rede:* attend to the advice; *snool:* cringe.

CHARLES DICKENS

LOUELLA C. POOLE

O to have known him, looked into his eyes,
    The music of his laughter to have heard!
How we would treasure as some dear won prize
    Were ours the memory of his spoken word!
Alas, for us such wish is futile, vain—
    Yet does he truly live for us today
In all those well-loved children of his brain
    That still companion us upon life's way,
So human, vital, how their presence e'er
    Breathes of the nature that did them conceive—
To charm, delight us, move to smile and tear,
    And round us spells of subtlest magic weave.
Aye, he shall ever live, so great his art,
Through all these children of his brain and heart!

They gather round us by the fireside—
    Sweet Nell, and Paul, poor Pip and Tiny Tim;
We meet them on life's journeys far and wide—
    Micawber, Pickwick, Betsy Trotwood grim,
His best-loved child, dear David Copperfield;
    And Oliver and Smike beset with fears—
How to their swift appeal our spirits yield,
    How do they move to laughter or to tears!
"Caricatures," you call them! Nay not so—
    Mankind as seen through comprehending eyes—
"Types," maybe, that we all of us do know,
    And knowing them can we not sympathize
(As did the tender heart within his breast)
More keenly with the suffering and oppressed?

He loved the masses; with their weal and woe
   His deep-felt sympathy was swift and sure;
To sham and falseness a relentless foe,
   He only scourged that he might help to cure.
His humor, genial as the noonday sun,
   Quickens our pulses like some cordial fine.
"The common people"—thus 'twas said of One,
   Our Master—"heard him gladly." By this sign,
And that he first loved us, how sure the sway
   Over our hearts our Dickens holds—his name
The magic "open sesame" today
   Of dear delights enduring as his fame;
And for that greatest gift, broad as the sea,
We love him most—his great humanity.

LINCOLN, THE MAN OF THE PEOPLE

Edwin Markham

When the Norn Mother saw the Whirlwind Hour
Greatening and darkening as it hurried on,
She left the Heaven of Heroes and came down
To make a man to meet the mortal need.
She took the tried clay of the common road—
Clay warm yet with the genial heat of Earth,
Dashed through it all a strain of prophecy;
Tempered the heap with thrill of human tears;
Then mixed a laughter with the serious stuff.
Into the shape she breathed a flame to light
That tender, tragic, ever-changing face,
And laid on him a sense of the Mystic Powers,
Moving—all hushed—behind the mortal veil.
Here was a man to hold against the world,
A man to match the mountains and the sea.

The color of the ground was in him, the red earth,
The smell and smack of elemental things:
The rectitude and patience of the cliff;
The good-will of the rain that loves all leaves;
The friendly welcome of the wayside well;
The courage of the bird that dares the sea;
The gladness of the wind that shakes the corn;
The pity of the snow that hides all scars;
The secrecy of streams that make their way
Under the mountain to the rifted rock;
The tolerance and equity of light
That gives as freely to the shrinking flower
As to the great oak flaring to the wind—
To the grave's low hill as to the Matterhorn
That shoulders out the sky. Sprung from the West
He drank the valorous youth of a new world.
The strength of virgin forests braced his mind;
The hush of spacious prairies stilled his soul.
His words were oaks in acorns; and his thoughts
Were roots that firmly gripped the granite truth.

Up from the log cabin to the Capitol,
One fire was on his spirit, one resolve—
To send the keen ax to the root of wrong,
Clearing a free way for the feet of God,
The eyes of conscience testing every stroke,
To make his deed the measure of a man.
He built the rail-pile as he built the State,
Pouring his splendid strength through every blow.
The grip that swung the ax in Illinois
Was on the pen that set a people free.

So came the Captain with the mighty heart;
And when the judgment thunders split the house,
Wrenching the rafters from their ancient rest,
He held the ridgepole up, and spiked again
The rafters of the Home. He held his place—
Held the long purpose like a growing tree—
Held on through blame and faltered not at praise.
And when he fell in whirlwind, he went down
As when a lordly cedar, green with boughs,
Goes down with a great shout upon the hills,
And leaves a lonesome place against the sky.

AT THE STEVENSON FOUNTAIN

Portsmouth Square, San Francisco

WALLACE IRWIN

Perhaps from out the thousands passing by—
  The City's hopeless lotus-eaters there,
  Blown by the four winds of the seven seas
From common want to common company—
Perhaps some one may lift a heavy eye
  And see, dream-blown across his memories,
  Those golden pennons bellying in the breeze
And spread for ports where fair adventure lies.

And oh, that such a one may stay a space
  And taste of sympathy, till to his ears
Might come the tale of him who knew the grace
  To suffer sweetly through the bitter years;
To catch the smile concealed in Fortune's face
  And draw contentment from a cup of tears!

NATURE AND HER MOODS

"GREEN-GIRDLED SPRING WAS AT THE WING, AND
WAITING FOR HER CUE!" (PAGE 189)

THE DÉBUTANTE

Guy Wetmore Carryl

To-day dawned not upon the earth as other days have done:
A throng of little virgin clouds stood waiting for the sun,
Till the herald-winds aligned them, and they blushed, and
   stood aside,
As the marshals of the morning flung the eastern portals
   wide.
So Nature lit her playhouse for the play that May begins,
And the twigs of honeysuckle sawed like little violins:
In the dawn there dwelt a whisper of a presence that was
   new,
For the slender Spring was at the wing, and waiting for her
   cue!

As yet I could not see her, and the stage was wide and
   bare;
As yet the Winter's chorus echoed faintly on the air
With a dying wail of tempest, and of dry and tortured trees,
But a promise of new music lent enchantment to the breeze.
In the scene's secluded corners lay the snowdrifts, still
   secure;
But the murmur of their melting sang another overture
Than the brooks of brown November, and I listened, and I
   knew
That blue-eyed Spring was at the wing, and waiting for her
   cue!

The world was all attention, and the hemlocks stood, a-row,
Ushers, never changing costume through the Season's wonder-
    show,
While the day, below the hillside, tried her colors, one by
    one,
On the clouds experimenting, till the coming of the sun.
In the vines about my window, where the sparrows all
    convene,
They were practicing the chorus that should usher in the
    Queen,
And the sod-imprisoned flowers craved the word to shoulder
    through:
Green-girdled Spring was at the wing, and waiting for her
    cue!

She shall enter to the clarion of the crystal-ringing brooks,
She shall tread on frail arbutus in the moist and mossy
    nooks;
She shall touch the bleak drop-curtain of the Winter with
    her wand
Till it lifts, and shows the wonder of the apple blooms
    beyond!
Yet with all her golden sunlight, and her twilights of perfume,
Yet with all the mystic splendor of her nights of starlit gloom,
She shall bring no sweeter moment than this one in which I
    knew
That laughing Spring was at the wing, and waiting for her
    cue!

THE WEATHER

Nancy Byrd Turner

Sometimes the weather is a man
   With gray cloak flying free;
His coat of mail is icy hail,
   A stormy steed rides he.
I cuddle in my bed at night
   With curtains gathered fast,
While just outside the window pane,
With clinking spur and rattling rein,
   He gallops, gallops past.

Sometimes the weather is a girl
   With eyes of bonny blue;
Gay flowers twined in every curl,
   Green buckles on each shoe;
Her mantle's wrought of shining gold,
   Her face is sweet with fun;
She reaches out and takes my hand,
And, laughing, through the happy land
   We run, run, run!

APRIL RAIN

Robert Loveman

It is not raining rain for me,
   It's raining daffodils;
In every dimpled drop I see
   Wild flowers on the hills.

The clouds of gray engulf the day
  And overwhelm the town;
It is not raining rain to me,
  It's raining roses down.

It is not raining rain to me,
  But fields of clover bloom,
Where any buccaneering bee
  Can find a bed and room.

A health unto the happy,
  A fig for him who frets!
It is not raining rain to me,
  It's raining violets.

THE WELCOME

ARTHUR POWELL

God spreads a carpet soft and green
  O'er which we pass;
A thick-piled mat of jeweled sheen—
  And that is Grass.

Delightful music woos the ear;
  The grass is stirred
Down to the heart of every spear—
  Ah, that's a Bird.

Clouds roll before a blue immense
  That stretches high
And lends the soul exalted sense—
  That scroll's a Sky.

Green rollers flaunt their sparkling crests;
   Their jubilee
Extols brave Captains and their quests—
   And that is Sea.

New-leaping grass, the feathery flute,
   The sapphire ring,
The sea's full-voiced, profound salute,—
   Ah, this is Spring!

A CHANT OUT OF DOORS[1]

MARGUERITE WILKINSON

God of grave nights,
God of brave mornings,
God of silent noon,
Hear my salutation!

  For where the rapids rage white and scornful,
  I have passed safely, filled with wonder;
  Where the sweet pools dream under willows,
  I have been swimming, filled with life.

God of round hills,
God of green valleys,
God of clear springs,
Hear my salutation!

  For where the moose feeds, I have eaten berries,
  Where the moose drinks, I have drunk deep.
  When the storm crashed through broken heavens—
  And under clear skies—I have known joy.

---

[1] Reprinted from Marguerite Wilkinson's "Bluestone." By special arrangement with The Macmillan Company, Publishers.

God of great trees,
God of wild grasses,
God of little flowers,
Hear my salutation!

For where the deer crops and the beaver plunges,
Near the river I have pitched my tent;
Where the pines cast aromatic needles
On a still floor, I have known peace.

God of grave nights,
God of brave mornings,
God of silent noon,
Hear my salutation!

A SONG IN SPRING

THOMAS S. JONES, Jr.

O little buds all bourgeoning with Spring,
    You hold my winter in forgetfulness;
Without my windows lilac branches swing,
Within my gate I hear a robin sing—
    O little laughing blooms that lift and bless!

So blow the breezes in a soft caress,
    Blowing my dreams upon a swallow's wing;
O little merry buds in dappled dress,
You fill my heart with very wantonness—
    O little buds all bourgeoning with Spring!

APRIL SPEAKS

Lloyd Mifflin

My pride is not in that I cause to bloom
  Each year the hawthorn by the cottage gate;
  Nor that I raise the rose's heart elate
With thoughts of climbing to my lady's room;
But that, one golden dawn, I did illume
  The world with him—a light to dominate
  And daze all time. It was my envied fate
To lay him in his cradle and his tomb.
When Nature gave him she became lovelorn,
  Nor would she let him longer here abide;
And if in memory of the time, men mourn,
  Grieving, "This is the day that Shakespeare died,"
  I, April, answer from the Avon-side,
"This is the day my dearest child was *born*!"

THE GREEN O' THE SPRING[1]

Denis Aloysius McCarthy

Sure, afther all the winther,
  An' afther all the snow,
'Tis fine to see the sunshine,
  'Tis fine to feel its glow;
'Tis fine to see the buds break
  On boughs that bare have been—
But best of all to Irish eyes
  'Tis grand to see the green!

---

[1] Copyrighted by Little, Brown & Company.

Sure, afther all the winther,
   An' afther all the snow,
'Tis fine to hear the brooks sing
   As on their way they go;
'Tis fine to hear at mornin'
   The voice of robineen,
But best of all to Irish eyes
   'Tis grand to see the green!

Sure, here in grim New England
   The spring is always slow,
An' every bit o' green grass
   Is kilt wid frost and snow;
Ah, many a heart is weary
   The winther days, I ween,
But oh, the joy when springtime comes
   An' brings the blessed green!

GYPSY-HEART

KATHARINE LEE BATES

The April world is misted with emerald and gold;
   The meadow larks are calling sweet and keen;
Gypsy-heart is up and off for woodland and for wold,
   Roaming, roaming, roaming through the green.
       Gypsy-heart, away!
    Oh, the wind—the wind and the sun!
Take the blithe adventure of the fugitive today;
   Youth will soon be done.

From buds that May is kissing there trembles forth a soul;
  The rosy boughs are whispering the white;
Gypsy-heart is heedless now of thrush and oriole
  Dreaming, dreaming, dreaming of delight.
      Gypsy-heart, beware!
    Oh, the song—the song in the blood!
  Magic walks the forest; there's bewitchment on the air.
      Spring is at the flood.

The wings of June are woven of fragrance and of fire;
  Heap roses, crimson roses for her throne.
Gypsy-heart is anguished with tumultuous desire,
  Seeking, seeking, seeking for its own.
      Gypsy-heart, abide!
    Oh, the far—the far is the near!
  'Tis a foolish fable that the universe is wide.
      All the world is here.

"AH, SWEET IS TIPPERARY"[1]

Denis Aloysius McCarthy

Ah, sweet is Tipperary in the springtime of the year,
  When the hawthorn's whiter than the snow,
When the feathered folk assemble and the air is all a-tremble
  With their singing and their winging to and fro;
When queenly Slieve-na-mon puts her verdant vesture on,
  And smiles to hear the news the breezes bring;
When the sun begins to glance on the rivulets that dance—
  Ah, sweet is Tipperary in the spring!

[1] Copyrighted by Little, Brown and Company.

Ah, sweet is Tipperary in the springtime of the year,
    When the mists are rising from the lea,
When the Golden Vale is smiling with a beauty all beguiling,
    And the Suir goes crooning to the sea;
When the shadows and the showers only multiply the flowers
    That the lavish hand of May will fling;
When in unfrequented ways, fairy music plays—
    Ah, sweet is Tipperary in the spring!

Ah, sweet is Tipperary in the springtime of the year,
    When life like the year is young,
When the soul is just awaking like a lily blossom breaking,
    And love words linger on the tongue;
When the blue of Irish skies is the hue of Irish eyes,
    And love-dreams cluster and cling
Round the heart and round the brain, half of pleasure, half
    of pain—
    Ah, sweet is Tipperary in the spring!

DA LEETLA BOY

Thomas Augustine Daly

Da spreeng ees com'; but oh, da joy
    Eet ees too late!
He was so cold, my leetla boy,
    He no could wait.

I no can count how manny week,
How manny day, dat he ees seeck;
How manny night I seet an' hold
Da leetla hand dat was so cold.

He was so patience, oh, so sweet!
Eet hurts my throat for theenk of eet;
An' all he evra ask ees w'en
Ees gona com' da spreeng agen.
Wan day, wan brighta sunny day,
He see, across da alleyway,
Da leetla girl dat's livin' dere
Ees raise her window for da air,
An' put outside a leetla pot
Of—w'at-you-call?—forgat-me-not.
So smalla flower, so leetla theeng!
But steell eet mak' hees hearta seeng;
"Oh, now, at las', ees com' da spreeng!
Da leetla plant ees glad for know
Da sun ees com' for mak' eet grow.
So, too, I am grow warm and strong."
So lika dat he seeng hees song.
But, ah, da night com' down an' den
Da weenter ees sneak back agen,
An' een da alley all da night
Ees fall da snow, so cold, so white,
An' cover up da leetla pot
Of—w'at-you-call?—forgat-me-not.
All night da leetla hand I hold
Ees grow so cold, so cold, so cold!

Da spreeng ees com'; but oh, da joy
   Eet ees too late!
He was so cold, my leetla boy,
   He no could wait.

"MAY IS BUILDING HER HOUSE"

RICHARD LE GALLIENNE

May is building her house. With apple blooms
She is roofing over the glimmering rooms;
  Of the oak and the beech hath she builded its beams,
And, spinning all day at her secret looms,
    With arras of leaves each wind-swayed wall
    She pictureth over, and peopleth it all
  With echoes and dreams,
  And singing of streams.

May is building her house of petal and blade;
Of the roots of the oak is the flooring made,
  With a carpet of mosses and lichen and clover,
  Each small miracle over and over,
And tender, traveling green things strayed.

Her windows, the morning and evening star,
And her rustling doorways, ever ajar
  With the coming and going
  Of fair things blowing,
The thresholds of the four winds are.

May is building her house. From the dust of things
She is making the songs and the flowers and the wings;
  From October's tossed and trodden gold
  She is making the young year out of the old;
    Yea: out of the winter's flying sleet
    She is making all the summer sweet,
    And the brown leaves spurned of November's feet
She is changing back again to spring's.

JUNE

Douglas Malloch

I knew that you were coming, June, I knew that you were
    coming!
Among the alders by the stream I heard a partridge
    drumming;
I heard a partridge drumming, June, a welcome with his
    wings,
And felt a softness in the air half Summer's and half Spring's.

I knew that you were nearing, June, I knew that you were
    nearing—
I saw it in the bursting buds of roses in the clearing;
The roses in the clearing, June, were blushing pink and red,
For they had heard upon the hills the echo of your tread.

I knew that you were coming, June, I knew that you were
    coming,
For ev'ry warbler in the wood a song of joy was humming.
I know that you are here, June, I know that you are here—
The fairy month, the merry month, the laughter of the year!

"WITH STRAWBERRIES"

William Ernest Henley

With strawberries we filled a tray,
And then we drove away, away
    Along the links beside the sea,
    Where wind and wave were light and free,
And August felt as fresh as May.

And where the springy turf was gay
With thyme and balm and many a spray
    Of wild roses, you tempted me
        With strawberries!

A shadowy sail, silent and grey,
Stole like a ghost across the bay;
    But none could hear me ask my fee,
    And none could know what came to be.
Can sweethearts *all* their thirst allay
        With strawberries?

A MIDSUMMER SONG

Richard Watson Gilder

O, Father's gone to market-town, he was up before the day,
And Jamie's after robins, and the man is making hay,
And whistling down the hollow goes the boy that minds the
    mill,
While mother from the kitchen-door is calling with a will:
    "Polly!—Polly!—The cows are in the corn!
        O, where's Polly?"

From all the misty morning air there comes a summer
    sound—
A murmur as of waters from skies and trees and ground.
The birds they sing upon the wing, the pigeons bill and coo,
And over hill and hollow rings again the loud halloo:
    "Polly!—Polly!—The cows are in the corn!
        O, where's Polly?"

Above the trees the honey-bees swarm by with buzz and
    boom,
And in the field and garden a thousand blossoms bloom.
Within the farmer's meadow a brown-eyed daisy blows,
And down at the edge of the hollow a red and thorny rose.
    But Polly!—Polly!—The cows are in the corn!
        O, where's Polly?

How strange at such a time of day the mill should stop its
    clatter!
The farmer's wife is listening now and wonders what's the
    matter.
O, wild the birds are singing in the wood and on the hill,
While whistling up the hollow goes the boy that minds the
    mill.
    But Polly!—Polly!—The cows are in the corn!
        O, where's Polly?

AT HUSKING TIME

E. Pauline Johnson

At husking time the tassel fades
To brown above the yellow blades
    Whose rustling sheath enswathes the corn
    That bursts its chrysalis, in scorn
Longer to lie in prison shades.

Among the merry lads and maids
The creaking ox-cart slowly wades
    'Twixt stalks and stubble, sacked, and torn
        At husking time.

The prying pilot crow persuades
The flock to join in thieving raids;
The sly racoon with craft inborn
His portion steals; from plenty's horn
His pouch the saucy chipmunk lades
At husking time.

"FROST TO-NIGHT"

Edith M. Thomas

Apple-green west and an orange bar,
And the crystal eye of a lone, one star . . .
And "Child, take the shears and cut what you will,
Frost to-night—so clear and dead-still."

Then I sally forth, half sad, half proud,
And I come to the velvet, imperial crowd,
The wine-red, the gold, the crimson, the pied,—
The dahlias that reign by the garden-side.

The dahlias I might not touch till to-night!
A gleam of the shears in the fading light,
And I gathered them all,—the splendid throng,
And in one great sheaf I bore them along.

In my garden of Life with its all late flowers
I heed a Voice in the shrinking hours:
"Frost to-night—so clear and dead-still" . . .
Half sad, half proud, my arms I fill.

NATURE'S MIRACLE

David Fallon

Autumn with chilling touch draws swiftly near;
Instant beneath that touch the land grows drear.
Silent, foreboding, comes the grey-toned day;
Only the leaves in hectic hues are gay.
Low o'er the barren hills the storm clouds loom,
And swift descending, fold the world in gloom.
The welcome rains beat down the land athirst;
O'erhead the threatening peals of thunder burst.
The heavy-laden air oppresses all;
Dry leaves seek shelter near the garden wall.
A few last flowers droop, wind-tossed and torn;
The birds fly south in terror, dumb, forlorn.
Robbed of her summer strength, earth somber lies
Affrighted, menaced by autumnal skies.
Dull days no color, sunshine, perfume hold;
All signs portend a winter bleak and cold.

Yet no blind fears distress the thoughtful soul.
Changes are marks of Nature's wise control.
This quick decay and seeming death, her way
To deck the world in next year's bright array.
That Spring may glorious break from Winter's tomb,
Ripe seeds lie hid beneath each fallen bloom;
And cushioned in brown shriveled stalks now rest
Those tiny leaves where Summer birds shall nest.
In folded beauty perfect there they wait
The call of warmth and light. Oh, happy state!
In peace and hope and confidence to rest
In sleep, upbuilding strength for God's behest!

Assured that Spring's first clarion song of bird
Shall waken all with new life richly stirred.
And joy, good-will, abounding love and faith
Shall ever triumph over wintry death!

THE CLOUD [1]

SARA TEASDALE

I am a cloud in the heaven's height,
The stars are lit for my delight,
Tireless and changeful, swift and free,
I cast my shadow on hill and sea—
But why do the pines on the mountain's crest
Call to me always, "Rest, rest"?

I throw my mantle over the moon
And I blind the sun on his throne at noon,
Nothing can tame me, nothing can bind,
I am a child of the heartless wind—
But oh, the pines on the mountain's crest
Whispering always, "Rest, rest."

SQUALL

LEONORA SPEYER

The squall swoops gray-winged across the obliterated hills,
And the startled lake seems to run before it;
From the wood comes a clamor of leaves,
Tugging at the twigs,
Pouring from the branches,
And suddenly the birds are still.

[1] Reprinted from Sara Teasdale's "Rivers to the Sea." By special
arrangement with The Macmillan Company, Publishers.

Thunder crumples the sky,
Lightning tears at it.

And now the rain!
The rain—thudding—implacable—
The wind, revelling in the confusion of great pines!

And a silver sifting of light,
A coolness;
A sense of summer anger passing,
Of summer gentleness creeping nearer—
Penitent, tearful,
Forgiven!

"I COME SINGING"

JOSEPH AUSLANDER

I come singing the keen sweet smell of grass
Cut after rain,
And the cool ripple of drops that pass
Over the grain,
And the drenched light drifting across the plain.

I come chanting the mad bloom of the fall.
And the swallows
Rallying in clans to the rapid call
From the hollows,
And the wet west wind swooping down on the swallows.

I come shrilling the sharp white of December,
The night like quick steel
Swung by a gust in its plunge through the pallid ember
Of dusk, and the heel
Of the fierce green dark grinding the stars like steel.

MONOTONE

CARL SANDBURG

The monotone of the rain is beautiful,
And the long sudden rise and the slow relapse
Of the long multitudinous rain.

The sun on the hills is beautiful,
Or a captured sunset, sea-flung,
Bannered with fire and gold.

A face I know is beautiful—
With fire and gold of sky and sea,
And the peace of the long warm rain.

"WIND-IN-THE-HAIR AND RAIN-IN-THE-FACE"

ARTHUR GUITERMAN

Wind-in-the-hair and Rain-in-the-face
  Are friends worth the having, and yours at command;
For many's the hour and many's the place
  We've frolicked together on ocean or land.

They'll brighten the darks of your gloomiest mood!
  They'll strengthen your heart with their boisterous play,
They'll buffet your anger until it's subdued,
  They'll sport with your sorrow and whisk it away.

Don't clutch in your curls with that grasp of despair!
  A tear on the cheek is a drop out of place!
"I'll rumple your tresses!" roars Wind-in-the-hair.
  "Let me do your crying!" trills Rain-in-the-face.

No seven-league boots like a pair of old shoes,
  No wish-cloak that equals a rain-beaded coat,
To take you away from the Realm of the Blues,
  To give you the will that grips Care by the throat!

How petty our griefs under God's open sky!
  How often but ghosts of a conjuring brain!
How quickly they dwindle, how lightly they fly,
  When winnowed and washed by the wind and the rain!

Then on with your shabbiest, hardiest wear!
  (The kind that the women-folk term "a disgrace!")
And swing down the highway with Wind-in-the-hair,
  Or splash through the puddles with Rain-in-the-face!

THE DAWN WIND

RUDYARD KIPLING

At two o'clock in the morning, if you open your window and
    listen,
  You will hear the feet of the Wind that is going to call the
    sun.
And the trees in the shadow rustle and the trees in the moon-
    light glisten,
  And though it is deep, dark night, you feel that the night is
    done.

So do the cows in the field. They graze for an hour and lie
    down,
  Dozing and chewing the cud; or a bird in the ivy wakes,
Chirrups one note and is still, and the restless Wind strays on,
  Fidgeting far down the road, till, softly, the silence breaks.

Back comes the Wind full strength with a blow like an angel's
    wing,
  Gentle but waking the world, as he shouts: "The Sun!
    The Sun!"
And the light floods over the fields and the birds begin to
    sing,
  And the Wind dies down in the grass. It is day and his
    work is done.

So when the world is asleep, and there seems no hope of her
    waking
  Out of some long, bad dream that makes her mutter and
    moan,
Suddenly, all men arise to the sound of fetters breaking,
  And every one smiles at his neighbor and tells him his soul
    is his own!

DAWN IN THE DESERT

Clinton Scollard

When the first opal presage of the morn
Quickened the east, the good Merwan arose,
And by his open tent door knelt and prayed.

Now in that pilgrim caravan was one
Whose heart was heavy with dumb doubts, whose eyes
Drew little balm from slumber. Up and down
Night-long he paced the avenues of sand
'Twixt tent and tent, and heard the jackals snarl,
The camels moan for water. This one came
On Merwan praying, and to him outcried—

(The tortured spirit bursting its sealed fount
As doth the brook on Damavend in spring)—
"How knowest thou that any Allah is?"
Swift from the sand did Merwan lift his face,
Flung toward the east an arm of knotted bronze.
And said, as upward shot a shaft of gold,
"Dost need a torch to show to thee the dawn?"
Then prayed again.

                When on the desert's rim
In sudden awful splendor stood the sun,
Through all that caravan there was no knee
But bowed to Allah.

AFTERNOON ON A HILL

Edna St. Vincent Millay

I will be the gladdest thing
    Under the sun!
I will touch a hundred flowers
    And not pick one.

I will look at cliffs and clouds
    With quiet eyes,
Watch the wind bow down the grass,
    And the grass rise.

And when lights begin to show
    Up from the town,
I will mark which must be mine,
    And then start down!

A PRAYER

Edwin Markham

Teach me, Father, how to go
Softly as the grasses grow;
Hush my soul to meet the shock
Of the wild world as a rock;
But my spirit, propped with power,
Make as simple as a flower.
Let the dry heart fill its cup,
Like a poppy looking up;
Let life lightly wear her crown,
Like a poppy looking down.

Teach me, Father, how to be
Kind and patient as a tree.
Joyfully the crickets croon
Under shady oak at noon;
Beetle, on his mission bent,
Tarries in that cooling tent.
Let me, also, cheer a spot,
Hidden field or garden grot—
Place where passing souls can rest
On their way and be their best.

NATURE'S FRIEND

William Henry Davies

Say what you like,
    All things love me!
I pick no flowers—
    That wins the Bee.

The Summer's Moths
  Think my hand one—
To touch their wings—
  With Wind and Sun.

The garden Mouse
  Comes near to play;
Indeed, he turns
  His eyes away.

The Wren knows well
  I rob no nest;
When I look in,
  She still will rest.

The hedge stops Cows,
  Or they would come
After my voice
  Right to my home.

The Horse can tell,
  Straight from my lip,
My hand could not
  Hold any whip.

Say what you like,
  All things love me!
Horse, Cow, and Mouse,
  Bird, Moth, and Bee.

THE LITTLE RED LARK

Katharine Tynan

The little red lark is shaking his wings,
Straight from the breast of his love he springs;
Listen the lilt of the song he sings,
    All in the morning early, O.

The sea is rocking a cradle, hark!
To a hushing-song, and the fields are dark,
And would I were there with the little red lark,
    All in the morning early, O.

The beard of barley is old-man's-gray,
All silver and green the new-mown hay;
The dew from his wings he has shaken away,
    All in the morning early, O.

The little red lark is high in the sky.
No eagle soars where the lark may fly.
Where are you going to, high, so high?
    All in the morning early, O.

His wings and feathers are sunrise red;
He hails the sun and his golden head:
"Good-morrow, Sun, you are long abed."
    All in the morning early, O.

I would I were where the little red lark
Up in the dawn like a rose-red spark,
Sheds the day on the fields so dark,
    All in the morning early, O.

THE MOCKING–BIRD

FRANK LEBBY STANTON

He didn't know much music
　　When first he come along;
An' all the birds went wonderin'
　　Why he didn't sing a song.

They primped their feathers in the sun,
　　An' sung their sweetest notes;
An' music jest come on the run
　　From all their purty throats!

But still that bird was silent
　　In summer time an' fall;
He jest set still an' listened,
　　An' he wouldn't sing at all!

But one night when them songsters
　　Was tired out an' still,
An' the wind sighed down the valley
　　An' went creepin' up the hill;

When the stars was all a-tremble
　　In the dreamin' fields o' blue,
An' the daisy in the darkness
　　Felt the fallin' o' the dew,—

There come a sound of melody
　　No mortal ever heard,
An' all the birds seemed singin'
　　From the throat o' one sweet bird!

Then the other birds went mayin'
    In a land too fur to call;
For there warn't no use in stayin'
    When one bird could sing for all!

THE BUTTERFLY

ALICE FREEMAN PALMER

I hold you at last in my hand,
    Exquisite child of the air.
Can I ever understand
    How you grew to be so fair?

You came to my linden tree
    To taste its delicious sweet,
I sitting here in the shadow and shine
    Playing around its feet.

Now I hold you fast in my hand,
    You marvelous butterfly,
Till you help me to understand
    The eternal mystery.

From that creeping thing in the dust
    To this shining bliss in the blue!
God give me courage to trust
    I can break my chrysalis too!

THE ROBIN IN THE RAIN

CHARLES COKE WOODS

Hear the robin in the rain;
Not one note doth he complain,
But he fills the storm's refrain
   With music of his own.

Drenched and drooped his finest feather,
Yet he sings in stormy weather;
Bird and God are glad together,
   A-singing in the rain.

That seer-songster's vision traces
Trails of light in darkest places,
Pouring through earth's stormy spaces
   The solace of his song.

ELLIS PARK

HELEN HOYT

Little park that I pass through,
I carry off a piece of you
Every morning hurrying down
To my work-day in the town;
Carry you for country there
To make the city ways more fair.
I take your trees,
And your breeze,
Your greenness,
Your cleanness,
Some of your shade, some of your sky,
Some of your calm as I go by;

Your flowers to trim
The pavements grim;
Your space for room in the jostled street
And grass for carpet to my feet.
Your fountains take and sweet bird calls
To sing me from my office walls.
All that I can see
I carry off with me.
But you never miss my theft,
So much treasure you have left.
As I find you, fresh at morning,
So I find you, home returning—
Nothing lacking from your grace.
All your riches wait in place
For me to borrow
On the morrow.
Do you hear this praise of you,
Little park that I pass through?

THE DRAGON-FLY

JESSIE BELLE RITTENHOUSE

The day was set to a beautiful theme
  By the blue of a dragon-fly
That poised with his airy wings agleam
  On a flower, as I passed by.

So frail and so lovely—a touch would destroy;
  He seemed but a fancy, a whim;
Yet this gossamer thing is a breath of God's joy,
  And Life is made perfect in him!

FOUR-LEAF CLOVER[1]

ELLA HIGGINSON

I know a place where the sun is like gold,
    And the cherry blossoms burst with snow,
And down underneath is the loveliest nook,
    Where the four-leaf clovers grow.

One leaf is for hope, and one is for faith,
    And one is for love, you know,
And God put another in for luck,—
    If you search, you will find where they grow.

But you must have hope, and you must have faith,
    You must love and be strong—and so,
If you work, if you wait, you will find the place
    Where the four-leaf clovers grow.

IN THE GRASS

HAMLIN GARLAND

O to lie in long grasses!
O to dream of the plain!
Where the west wind sings as it passes
A weird and unceasing refrain;
Where the rank grass wallows and tosses,
And the plains' ring dazzles the eye;
Where hardly a silver cloud bosses
The flashing steel arch of the sky.

[1] Reprinted from Ella Higginson's "When the Birds Go North Again."
By special arrangement with The Macmillan Company, Publishers.

To watch the gay gulls as they flutter
Like snowflakes and fall down the sky,
To swoop in the deeps of the hollows,
Where the crow's-foot tosses awry,
And gnats in the lee of the thickets
Are swirling like waltzers in glee
To the harsh, shrill creak of the crickets,
And the sound of the lark and the bee.

O far-off plains of my west land!
O lands of winds and the free
Swift deer—my mist-clad plain!
From my bed in the heart of the forest,
From the clasp and the girdle of pain,
Your light through my darkness passes;
To your meadows in dreaming I fly
To plunge in the deeps of your grasses,
To bask in the light of your sky.

SYMBOL[1]

DAVID MORTON

My faith is all a doubtful thing,
    Wove on a doubtful loom,—
Until there comes, each showery Spring,
    A cherry-tree in bloom;

And Christ who died upon a tree
    That death had stricken bare,
Comes beautifully back to me,
    In blossoms, everywhere.

[1] From "Ships in Harbour," by David Morton. Courtesy of G. P. Putnam's Sons, Publishers, New York and London.

"LOVELIEST OF TREES"

Alfred Edward Housman

Loveliest of trees, the cherry now
Is hung with bloom along the bough,
And stands about the woodland ride
Wearing white for Eastertide.

Now, of my threescore years and ten,
Twenty will not come again,
And take from seventy springs a score,
It only leaves me fifty more.

And since to look at things in bloom
Fifty springs are little room,
About the woodlands I will go
To see the cherry hung with snow.

GOOD COMPANY

Karle Wilson Baker

To-day I have grown taller from walking with the trees,
   The seven sister-poplars who go softly in a line;
And I think my heart is whiter for its parley with a star
   That trembled out at nightfall and hung above the pine.

The call-note of a redbird from the cedars in the dusk
   Woke his happy mate within me to an answer free and fine;
And a sudden angel beckoned from a column of blue
    smoke—
    Lord, who am I that they should stoop—these holy folk of
    thine?

TREES[1]

JOYCE KILMER

I think that I shall never see
A poem lovely as a tree.

A tree whose hungry mouth is prest
Against the earth's sweet flowing breast;

A tree that looks at God all day,
And lifts her leafy arms to pray;

A tree that may in summer wear
A nest of robins in her hair;

Upon whose bosom snow has lain;
Who intimately lives with rain.

Poems are made by fools like me,
But only God can make a tree.

THE MOUNTAINS ARE A LONELY FOLK

HAMLIN GARLAND

The mountains are a silent folk;
    They stand afar—alone,
And the clouds that kiss their brows at night
    Hear neither sigh nor groan.
Each bears him in his ordered place
    As soldiers do, and bold and high
They fold their forests round their feet
    And bolster up the sky.

[1] From "Trees and Other Poems," by Joyce Kilmer.   Copyright,
1914, by George H. Doran Company, Publishers.

"THE SEA IS WILD"

JOHN HALL WHEELOCK

The sea is wild and flecked with white,
  The dunes lean dumb and drear,
Something familiar in the sight
  Thrills me a moment here.

The darkness and the salt sea's tang,
  They stab me through and through
With ecstasy,—the sharp, sweet pang
  And memory of you.

THE SHELL[1]

JAMES STEPHENS

And then I pressed the shell
Close to my ear
And listened well,
And straightway like a bell
Came low and clear
The slow, sad murmur of the distant seas,
Whipped by an icy breeze
Upon a shore
Wind-swept and desolate.
It was a sunless strand that never bore
The footprint of a man,
Nor felt the weight
Since time began

[1] Reprinted from James Stephens's "Insurrections." By special arrangement with The Macmillan Company, Publishers.

Of any human quality or stir
Save what the dreary winds and waves incur.
And in the hush of waters was the sound
Of pebbles rolling round,
Forever rolling with a hollow sound.
And bubbling sea-weeds as the waters go
Swish to and fro
Their long, cold tentacles of slimy gray.
There was no day,
Nor ever came a night
Setting the stars alight
To wonder at the moon;
Was twilight only and the frightened croon,
Smitten to whispers, of the dreary wind
And waves that journeyed blind—
And then I loosed my ear. . . . O, it was sweet
To hear a cart go jolting down the street.

HOPE AND HIGH ENDEAVOR

"OLD LAMPS FOR NEW?" (PAGE 238)

"WHERE ARE YOU GOING, GREAT-HEART?" [1]

John Oxenham

Where are you going, Great-Heart,
With your eager face and your fiery grace?—
Where are you going, Great-Heart?

"To fight a fight with all my might,
For Truth and Justice, God and Right,
To grace all Life with His fair Light."
Then God go with you, Great-Heart!

Where are you going, Great-Heart?
"To beard the Devil in his den;
To smite him with the strength of ten;
To set at large the souls of men."
Then God go with you, Great-Heart!

Where are you going, Great-Heart?
"To end the rule of knavery;
To break the yoke of slavery;
To give the world delivery."
Then God go with you, Great-Heart!

[1] From "The Vision Splendid," by John Oxenham. Copyright, 1917, by George H. Doran Company, Publishers.

Where are you going, Great-Heart?
　　"To hurl high-stationed evil down;
　　To set the Cross above the crown;
　　To spread abroad my King's renown."
　　　Then God go with you, Great-Heart!

Where are you going, Great-Heart?
　　"To cleanse the earth of noisome things;
　　To draw from life its poison-stings;
　　To give free play to Freedom's wings."
　　　Then God go with you, Great-Heart!

Where are you going, Great-Heart?
　　"To lift To-day above the Past;
　　To make To-morrow sure and fast;
　　To nail God's colors to the mast."
　　　Then God go with you, Great-Heart!

Where are you going, Great-Heart?
　　"To break down old dividing-lines;
　　To carry out my Lord's designs;
　　To build again His broken shrines."
　　　Then God go with you, Great-Heart!

Where are you going, Great-Heart?
　　"To set all burdened peoples free;
　　To win for all God's liberty;
　　To 'stablish His sweet sovereignty."
　　　God goeth with you, Great-Heart!

IF

Rudyard Kipling

If you can keep your head when all about you
   Are losing theirs and blaming it on you,
If you can trust yourself when all men doubt you,
   But make allowance for their doubting too;
If you can wait and not be tired by waiting,
   Or being lied about don't deal in lies,
Or being hated don't give way to hating,
   And yet don't look too good, nor talk too wise:

If you can dream—and not make dreams your master;
   If you can think—and not make thoughts your aim,
If you can meet with Triumph and Disaster
   And treat these two impostors just the same;
If you can bear to hear the truth you've spoken
   Twisted by knaves to make a trap for fools,
Or watch the things you gave your life to, broken,
   And stoop and build 'em up with worn-out tools:

If you can make one heap of all your winnings
   And risk it on one turn of pitch-and-toss,
And lose, and start again at your beginnings
   And never breathe a word about your loss;
If you can force your heart and nerve and sinew
   To serve your turn long after they are gone,
And so hold on when there is nothing in you
   Except the will which says to them: "Hold on!"

If you can talk with crowds and keep your virtue,
  Or walk with Kings—nor lose the common touch,
If neither foes nor loving friends can hurt you,
  If all men count with you, but none too much;
If you can fill the unforgiving minute
  With sixty seconds' worth of distance run,
Yours is the Earth and everything that's in it,
  And—which is more—you'll be a Man, my son!

"IF I HAD YOUTH"[1]

Edgar A. Guest

If I had youth, I'd bid the world to try me;
  I'd answer every challenge to my will;
And though the silent mountains should defy me,
  I'd try to make them subject to my skill.
I'd keep my dreams and follow where they led me;
  I'd glory in the hazards which abound;
I'd eat the simple fare privations fed me,
  And gladly make my couch upon the ground.

If I had youth, I'd ask no odds of distance,
  Nor wish to tread the known and level ways,
I'd want to meet and master strong resistance,
  And in a worth-while struggle spend my days.
I'd see the task which calls for full endeavor;
  I'd feel the thrill of battle in my veins,
I'd bear my burden gallantly, and never
  Desert the hills to walk on common plains.

[1] From "When Day is Done." Copyright, 1919, by The Reilly and Lee Company.

If I had youth, no thought of failure lurking
  Beyond to-morrow's dawn should fright my soul.
Let failure strike—it still would find me working
  With faith that I should some day reach my goal.
I'd dice with danger—aye!—and glory in it;
  I'd make high stakes the purpose of my throw.
I'd risk for much, and should I fail to win it,
  I would never even whimper at the blow.

If I had youth, no chains of fear should bind me;
  I'd brave the heights which older men must shun.
I'd leave the well-worn lanes of life behind me,
  And seek to do what men have never done.
Rich prizes wait for those who do not waver;
  The world needs men to battle for the truth.
It calls each hour for stronger hearts and braver.
  This is the age for those who still have youth!

A PRAYER

Frank Dempster Sherman

It is my joy in life to find
  At every turning of the road,
The strong arm of a comrade kind
  To help me onward with my load.

And since I have no gold to give,
  And love alone must make amends,
My only prayer is, while I live,—
  God make me worthy of my friends!

THE PLAN

Richard Burton

The peoples in their peril and their pain
Cry out, cry on, and ever cry again
Against the hate and horrors of the hours
Where war and wasting crucify men's powers. . . .

Yet, in my garden where the May is host,
She walks in Beauty, and the Pentecost
Turns to a feast, a rioting of song,
A festa, pink and white, the paths along.

The happy rhythm of the inner things—
In bloom and bush and bird on irised wings—
Seems still to whisper of a coming time
When sphere with sphere shall in their motion chime;

When brother shall with brother walk in peace,
Watching the kindly fruits of earth increase;
And all the energies beneath the dome
Shall find the harmony that roots in Home—

Which is the deeper reading of the Plan
More ancient than the ancientest of man:
Red revolution on a Devil's day,
Or riant blossoms on a morn of May?

A SONG OF LIVING[1]

AMELIA JOSEPHINE BURR

Because I have loved life, I shall have no sorrow to die.
I have sent up my gladness on wings, to be lost in the blue
  of the sky,
I have run and leaped with the rain, I have taken the wind to
  my breast.
My cheek like a drowsy child to the face of the earth I have
  pressed.
Because I have loved life, I shall have no sorrow to die.

I have kissed young Love on the lips, I have heard his song
  to the end.
I have struck my hand like a seal in the loyal hand of a
  friend.
I have known the peace of heaven, the comfort of work done
  well.
I have longed for death in the darkness and risen alive out of
  hell.
Because I have loved life, I shall have no sorrow to die.

I give a share of my soul to the world where my course is
  run.
I know that another shall finish the task I must leave un-
  done.
I know that no flower, no flint was in vain on the path I trod.
As one looks on a face through a window, through life I have
  looked on God.
Because I have loved life, I shall have no sorrow to die.

[1] From "Life and Living," by Amelia Josephine Burr. Copyright,
1916, by George H. Doran Company, Publishers.

SONG OF LIFE

Florence Earle Coates

Maiden of the laughing eyes,
  Primrose-kirtled, wingèd, free,
Virgin daughter of the skies—
Joy—whom gods and mortals prize,
  Share thy smiles with me!

Yet—lest I, unheeding, borrow
  Pleasure that today endears,
And benumbs the heart to-morrow—
Turn not wholly from me, Sorrow!
  Let me share thy tears!

Give me of thy fulness, Life!
  Pulse and passion, power, breath,
Vision pure, heroic strife—
Give me of thy fulness, Life!
  Nor deny me death!

WINDOWS

Abbie Farwell Brown

The windows of the place wherein I dwell
  I will make beautiful. No garish light
  Shall enter crudely; but with colors bright
And warm and throbbing I will weave a spell,
In rainbow harmony the theme to tell
  Of sage and simple saint and noble knight,
  Beggar and king who fought the gallant fight.
These will transfigure even my poor cell.

But when the shadows of the night begin,
  And sifted sunlight falls no more on me,
May I have learned to light my lamp within;
  So that the passing world may look and see
Still the same radiance, though with paler hue,
Of the sweet lives that help men to live true.

BALLADE BY THE FIRE

Edwin Arlington Robinson

Slowly I smoke and hug my knee,
  The while a witless masquerade
Of things that only children see
  Floats in a mist of light and shade:
  They pass, a flimsy cavalcade,
And with a weak, remindful glow,
  The falling embers break and fade,
As one by one the phantoms go.

Then, with a melancholy glee
  To think where once my fancy strayed,
I muse on what the years may be
  Whose coming tales are all unsaid,
  Till tongs and shovel, snugly laid
Within their shadowed niches, grow
  By dim degrees to pick and spade,
As one by one the phantoms go.

But then, what though the mystic Three
  Around me ply their merry trade?—
And Charon soon may carry me
  Across the gloomy Stygian glade?—

Be up, my soul; nor be afraid
Of what some unborn year may show;
　But mind your human debts are paid,
As one by one the phantoms go.

ENVOY

Life is the game that must be played:
　This truth at least, good friends, we know;
So live and laugh, nor be dismayed
　As one by one the phantoms go.

ALMS

Josephine Preston Peabody

I met Poor Sorrow on the way
　As I came down the years;
I gave him everything I had
　And looked at him through tears.

"But Sorrow, give me here again
　Some little sign to show;
For I have given all I own;
　Yet have I far to go."

Then Sorrow charmed my eyes for me
　And hallowed them thus far:
"Look deep enough in every dark,
　And you shall see the star."

SOMETIMES

Thomas S. Jones, Jr.

Across the fields of yesterday
  He sometimes comes to me,
A little lad just back from play—
  The lad I used to be.

And yet he smiles so wistfully
  Once he has crept within,
I wonder if he hopes to see
  The man I might have been.

BY AN OPEN WINDOW IN CHURCH

Corinne Roosevelt Robinson

I hear the music of the murmuring breeze,
  It mingles with the preacher's quiet word;
  Dim, holy memories are waked and stirred,
I seem to touch once more my mother's knees.
Christ's human love, His spirit mysteries
  Envelop me. It is as though I heard
  An angel choir in the singing bird
That floats above the fair full-foliaged trees.
The old sweet Faith is singing at my breast
  With peace in Nature's summer subtly blent,
  All of my being breathes a deep content—
Life and its unremitting, baffled quest
Fade into this rich sense of perfect rest—
  My soul, renewed, is steeped in sacrament.

BLIND

Harry Kemp

The Spring blew trumpets of color;
  Her Green sang in my brain . . .
I heard a blind man groping
  "Tap-tap" with his cane;

I pitied him in his blindness;
  But can I boast, "I see"?
Perhaps there walks a spirit
  Close by, who pities me,—

A spirit who hears me tapping
  The five-sensed cane of mind
Amid such unguessed glories—
  That I—am worse than blind!

OLD BOOKS FOR NEW

Edwin Francis Edgett

Through the streets and bazaars
Of a far Eastern city
There went one day a Moor
Bearing in a basket
A glittering array of lamps.
And as he walked he cried:
"Oh, who will give
Old lamps for new?"
And all the world followed him
And the street boys pursued him

From place to place,
And mocked at him.
But he cared not for that,
For when he reached
The palace of Ala-ed Din
He gained the prize he sought,
The Magical Lamp of the Treasure,
In exchange for his tawdry wares.

And so today
In Western lands
Great thoughts out of the past
Woven from the magic of men's minds
Are bartered or are cast aside
Whenever we are asked to give
Old books for new.

MY CREED

HOWARD ARNOLD WALTER

I would be true, for there are those who trust me;
  I would be pure, for there are those who care;
I would be strong, for there is much to suffer;
  I would be brave, for there is much to dare.

I would be friend of all—the foe, the friendless;
  I would be giving and forget the gift;
I would be humble, for I know my weakness;
  I would look up—and laugh—and love—and lift.

"AS IN A ROSE–JAR"

Thomas S. Jones, Jr.

As in a rose-jar filled with petals sweet
    Blown long ago in some old garden place,
    Mayhap, where you and I, a little space
Drank deep of love and knew that love was fleet—
Or leaves once gathered from a lost retreat
    By one who never will again retrace
    Her silent footsteps—one, whose gentle face
Was fairer than the roses at her feet;

So deep within the vase of memory
    I keep my dust of roses fresh and dear
        As in the days before I knew the smart
Of time and death. Nor aught can take from me
    The haunting fragrance that still lingers here—
        As in a rose-jar, so within the heart!

IMMORTALITY

Lizette Woodworth Reese

Battles nor songs can from oblivion save,
    But Fame upon a white deed loves to build;
From out that cup of water Sidney gave,
    Not one drop has been spilled.

EACH IN HIS OWN TONGUE[1]

WILLIAM HERBERT CARRUTH

A fire-mist and a planet,—
    A crystal and a cell,—
A jellyfish and a saurian,
    And caves where the cave-men dwell;
Then a sense of law and beauty,
    And a face turned from the clod,—
Some call it Evolution,
    And others call it God.

A haze on the far horizon,
    The infinite, tender sky,
The ripe, rich tint of the cornfields,
    And the wild geese sailing high,—
And all over upland and lowland
    The charm of the goldenrod,—
Some of us call it Autumn,
    And others call it God.

Like tides on a crescent sea-beach,
    When the moon is new and thin,
Into our hearts high yearnings
    Come welling and surging in,—
Come from the mystic ocean,
    Whose rim no foot has trod,—
Some of us call it Longing,
    And others call it God.

[1] From "Each in His Own Tongue," by William Herbert Carruth. Courtesy of G. P. Putnam's Sons, Publishers, New York and London.

A picket frozen on duty,—
    A mother starved for her brood,—
Socrates drinking the hemlock,
    And Jesus on the rood;
And millions who, humble and nameless,
    The straight, hard pathway plod,—
Some call it Consecration,
    And others call it God.

THE VOICE OF CHRISTMAS

Harry Kemp

I cannot put the Presence by, of Him, the Crucified,
Who moves men's spirits with His Love as doth the moon the
    tide;
Again I see the Life He lived, the godlike Death He died.

Again I see upon the cross that great Soul-battle fought,
Into the texture of the world the tale of which is wrought
Until it hath become the woof of human deed and thought,—

And, joining with the cadenced bells that all the morning fill,
His cry of agony doth yet my inmost being thrill,
Like some fresh grief from yesterday that tears the heart-
    strings still.

I cannot put His Presence by, I meet Him everywhere;
I meet Him in the country town, the busy market-square;
The Mansion and the Tenement attest His Presence there.

Upon the funneled ships at sea He sets His shining feet;
The Distant Ends of Empire not in vain His Name repeat,—
And, like the presence of a rose, He makes the whole world
    sweet.

He comes to break the barriers down raised up by barren
    creeds;
About the globe from zone to zone like sunlight He proceeds;
He comes to give the World's starved heart the perfect love it
    needs,

The Christ, Whose friends have played Him false, Whom
    Dogmas have belied,
Still speaking to the hearts of men—though shamed and
    crucified,
The Master of the Centuries Who will not be denied!

"DE MASSA OB DE SHEEPFOL'"

SARAH PRATT McLEAN GREENE

De massa ob de sheepfol'
    Dat guards de sheepfol' bin,
Look out in de gloomerin' meadows
    Wha'r de long night rain begin—
So he call to de hirelin' shepha'd:
    "Is my sheep—is dey all come in?
    My sheep, is dey all come in?"

Oh den says de hirelin' shepha'd,
    "Dey's some, dey's black and thin,
And some, dey's po' ol' wedda's—
    Dat can't come home agin.

Dey's some black sheep an' ol' wedda's,
　　But de res', dey's all brung in.—
　　De res', dey's all brung in."

Den de massa ob de sheepfol'
　　Dat guards de sheepfol' bin,
Goes down in de gloomerin' meadows
Wha'r de long night rain begin—
So he le' down de ba's ob de sheepfol',
　　Callin' sof': "Come in! Come in!"
　　Callin' sof': "Come in! Come in!"

Den up t'ro' de gloomerin' meadows,
　　T'ro' de col' night rain an' win',
And up t'ro' de gloomerin' rain-paf'
　　Wha'r de sleet fa' piercin' thin,
De po' los' sheep ob de sheepfol',
　　Dey all comes gadderin' in.
De po' los' sheep ob de sheepfol',
　　Dey all comes gadderin' in!

TO A POET A THOUSAND YEARS HENCE

JAMES ELROY FLECKER

I who am dead a thousand years,
　　And wrote this sweet archaic song,
Send you my words for messengers
　　The way I shall not pass along.

I care not if you bridge the seas,
　　Or ride secure the cruel sky,
Or build consummate palaces
　　Of metal or of masonry.

But have you wine and music still,
    And statues and a bright-eyed love,
And foolish thoughts of good and ill,
    And prayers to them that sit above?

How shall we conquer? Like a wind
    That falls at eve our fancies blow,
And old Mæonides the blind
    Said it three thousand years ago.

O friend unseen, unborn, unknown,
    Student of our sweet English tongue,
Read out my words at night, alone:
    I was a poet, I was young.

Since I can never see your face,
    And never shake you by the hand,
I send my soul through time and space
    To greet you. You will understand.

THE POET

INA DONNA COOLBRITH

He walks with God upon the hills!
    And sees, each morn, the world arise
    New-bathed in light of paradise.
He learns the laughter of her rills,
    Her melodies of many voices,
    And greets her while his heart rejoices.
She, to his spirit undefiled,
Makes answer as a little child;
    Unveiled before his eyes she stands
    And gives her secrets to his hands.

"IN AFTER DAYS"

Austin Dobson

In after days when grasses high
O'er-top the stone where I shall lie,
 Though ill or well the world adjust
 My slender claim to honored dust,
I shall not question or reply.

I shall not see the morning sky;
I shall not hear the night-wind sigh;
 I shall be mute, as all men must
  In after days!

But yet, now living, fain were I
That some one then should testify,
 Saying—"He held his pen in trust
 To Art, not serving shame or lust."
Will none?—Then let my memory die
  In after days!

INVICTUS

William Ernest Henley

Out of the night that covers me,
 Black as the pit from pole to pole,
I thank whatever gods there be
 For my unconquerable soul.

In the fell clutch of circumstance
 I have not winced nor cried aloud.

Beneath the bludgeonings of chance
    My head is bloody, but unbowed.

Beyond this space of wrath and tears
    Looms but the Horror of the shade,
And yet the menace of the years
    Finds and shall find me unafraid.

It matters not how strait the gate,
    How charged with punishments the scroll,
I am the master of my fate:
    I am the captain of my soul.

"HE WHOM A DREAM HATH POSSESSED"

SHAEMAS O'SHEEL

He whom a dream hath possessed knoweth no more of
    doubting,
    For mist and the blowing of winds and the mouthing of
    words he scorns;
Not the sinuous speech of schools he hears, but a knightly
    shouting,
    And never comes darkness down, yet he greeteth a million
    morns.

He whom a dream hath possessed knoweth no more of
    roaming;
    All roads and the flowing of waves and the speediest flight
    he knows,
But wherever his feet are set, his soul is forever homing,
    And going, he comes, and coming he heareth a call and
    goes.

He whom a dream hath possessed knoweth no more of sorrow,
  At death and the dropping of leaves and the fading of suns
    he smiles,
For a dream remembers no past and scorns the desire of a
    morrow,
  And a dream in a sea of doom sets surely the ultimate isles.

He whom a dream hath possessed treads the implacable
    marches,
  From the dust of the day's long road he leaps to a laughing
    star,
And the ruin of worlds that fall he views from eternal arches,
  And rides God's battlefield in a flashing and golden car.

THE WILD RIDE

Louise Imogen Guiney

I hear in my heart, I hear in its ominous pulses
All day, on the road, the hoofs of invisible horses,
All night, from their stalls, the importunate pawing and
    neighing.

Let cowards and laggards fall back! but alert to the saddle
Weatherworn and abreast, go men of our galloping legion,
With a stirrup-cup each to the lily of women that loves him.

The trail is through dolor and dread, over crags and
    morasses;
There are shapes by the way, there are things that appal or
    entice us:
What odds? We are Knights of the Grail, we are vowed to
    the riding.

Thought's self is a vanishing wing, and joy is a cobweb,
And friendship a flower in the dust, and glory a sunbeam:
Not here is our prize, nor, alas! after these our pursuing.

A dipping of plumes, a tear, a shake of the bridle,
A passing salute to this world and her pitiful beauty:
We hurry with never a word in the track of our fathers.

I hear in my heart, I hear in its ominous pulses
All day, on the road, the hoofs of invisible horses,
All night, from their stalls, the importunate pawing and
neighing.

We spur to a land of no name, outracing the storm-wind;
We leap to the infinite dark like sparks from the anvil,
Thou leadest, O God! All's well with Thy troopers that
follow.

THE FALCONER OF GOD

WILLIAM ROSE BENÉT

I flung my soul to the air like a falcon flying.
I said, "Wait on, wait on, while I ride below!
     I shall start a heron soon
     In the marsh beneath the moon—
A strange white heron rising with silver on its wings,
          Rising and crying
     Wordless, wondrous things;
The secret of the stars, of the world's heart-strings
     The answer to their woe.
Then stoop thou upon him, and grip him and hold him so!"

My wild soul waited on as falcons hover.
I beat the reedy fens as I trampled past.
 I heard the mournful loon
 In the marsh beneath the moon.
And then with feathery thunder—the bird of my desire
  Broke from the cover
 Flashing silver fire.
High up among the stars I saw his pinions spire.
 The pale clouds gazed aghast
As my falcon stooped upon him, and gripped and held him fast.

My soul dropped through the air—with heavenly plunder?—
Gripping the dazzling bird my dreaming knew?
 Nay! but a piteous freight,
 A dark and heavy weight
Despoiled of silver plumage, its voice forever stilled,—
  All of the wonder
 Gone that ever filled
Its guise with glory. Oh, bird that I have killed,
 How brilliantly you flew
Across my rapturous vision when first I dreamed of you!

Yet I fling my soul on high with new endeavor,
And I ride the world below with a joyful mind.
 I shall start a heron soon
 In the marsh beneath the moon—
A wondrous silver heron its inner darkness fledges!
 I beat forever
 The fens and the sedges.
The pledge is still the same—for all disastrous pledges,
 All hopes resigned!
My soul still flies above me for the quarry it shall find.

THE PEAK

Mary Carolyn Davies

There's a far high trail where the pines are,
  There's a gray faint trail to the dawn,
There's a sudden hush on the hillside—
  Look! The last star's gone!
And, follow, follow, the far trail seems to say,
Follow, comrade, follow, and you'll make the peak to-day!

There's a steep hard trail where the stones are,
  There's a sharp crag gray at the bend;
There's a far fine mist where the road winds—
  What is at the end?
Follow, follow, the dark trail seems to say,
Follow, comrade, follow, and you'll make the peak to-day!

There's an unknown trail—but we'll take it.
  It's a steep hard trail—who's afraid?
There are deep sharp chasms to walk by;
  No one's hands can aid.
Follow, follow, the far trail seems to say,
Follow, comrade, follow, and you'll make the peak to-day!

A MILE WITH ME

Henry van Dyke

O who will walk a mile with me
  Along life's merry way?
A comrade blithe and full of glee,
Who dares to laugh out loud and free,

And let his frolic fancy play,
Like a happy child, through the flowers gay
That fill the field and fringe the way
   Where he walks a mile with me.

And who will walk a mile with me
   Along life's weary way?
A friend whose heart has eyes to see
The stars shine out o'er the darkening lea,
And the quiet rest at the end o' the day,—
A friend who knows, and dares to say,
The brave, sweet words that cheer the way
   Where he walks a mile with me.

With such a comrade, such a friend,
I fain would walk till journeys end,
Through summer sunshine, winter rain,
And then?—Farewell, we shall meet again!

THE HILLS OF REST

Albert Bigelow Paine

Beyond the last horizon's rim,
   Beyond adventure's farthest quest,
Somewhere they rise, serene and dim,
   The happy, happy Hills of Rest.

Upon their sunlit slopes uplift
   The castles we have built in Spain—
While fair amid the summer drift
   Our faded gardens flower again.

Sweet hours we did not live go by
   To soothing note, on scented wing;
In golden-lettered volumes lie
   The songs we tried in vain to sing.

They are all there: the days of dream
   That build the inner lives of men;
The silent, sacred years we deem
   The might be, and the might have been.

Some evening when the sky is gold
   I'll follow day into the west;
Nor pause, nor heed, till I behold
   The happy, happy Hills of Rest.

A PARTING GUEST[1]

JAMES WHITCOMB RILEY

What delightful hosts are they—
   Life and Love!
Lingeringly I turn away,
   This late hour, yet glad enough
They have not withheld from me
   Their high hospitality.
So, with face lit with delight
   And all gratitude, I stay
   Yet to press their hands and say,
"Thanks.—So fine a time! Good night."

GOD'S GIFT

Alfred Noyes

There's but one gift that all our dead desire,
  One gift that men can give and that's a dream,
Unless we, too, can burn with that same fire
  Of sacrifice; die to the things that seem;

Die to the little hatreds; die to greed;
  Die to the old ignoble selves we knew;
Die to the base contempts of sect and creed,
  And rise again, like these, with souls as true.

Nay (since these died before their tasks were finished)
  Attempt new heights, bring even their dreams to birth:—
Build us that better world, O, not diminished
  By one true splendor that they planned on earth.

And that's not done by sword, or tongue, or pen.
There's but one way. God make us better men.

ENVOY[1]

Francis Thompson

Go, songs, for ended is our brief, sweet play;
  Go, children of swift joy and tardy sorrow:
And some are sung, and that was yesterday,
  And some unsung, and that may be to-morrow.

[1] Reprinted by special arrangement with Mr. Thompson's London
publishers, Messrs. Burns, Oates, and Washbourne.

Go forth; and if it be o'er stony way,
    Old joy can lend what newer grief must borrow:
And it was sweet, and that was yesterday,
And sweet is sweet, though purchasèd with sorrow.

Go, songs, and come not back from your far way:
    And if men ask you why ye smile and sorrow,
Tell them ye grieve, for your hearts know To-day,
    Tell them ye smile, for your eyes know To-morrow.

"WHEN EARTH'S LAST PICTURE IS PAINTED"

RUDYARD KIPLING

When Earth's last picture is painted, and the tubes are
    twisted and dried,
When the oldest colors have faded, and the youngest critic
    has died,
We shall rest, and, faith, we shall need it—lie down for an
    æon or two,
Till the Master of All Good Workmen shall put us to work
    anew!

And those that were good shall be happy: they shall sit in
    a golden chair;
They shall splash at a ten-league canvas with brushes of
    comet's hair;
They shall find real saints to draw from—Magdalene, Peter,
    and Paul;
They shall work for an age at a sitting and never be tired
    at all!

And only the Master shall praise us, and only the Master
 shall blame;
And no one shall work for money, and no one shall work for
 fame;
But each for the joy of the working, and each, in his
 separate star,
Shall draw the Thing as he sees It for the God of Things as
 They are!

THE FORM OF POETRY

Poetry differs from prose in its deliberate rhythm—the particular march or swing of its lines. Through the definite rhythmic movement, the musical words, and the beauty of imagery it awakens our higher emotions and helps us to a truer appreciation of the meaning of life. The poet paints pictures of beauty and truth in words of imperishable power and melody. An acquaintance with the structures upon which poets build is a real aid in the appreciation of their work. In the hope of increasing the reader's delight in poetry, a few of these forms are presented here.

RHYTHM

Rhythm, the quality which distinguishes poetry from prose, is the regular recurrence of accented syllables. This alternation of accented and unaccented syllables gives the beat of the line.

The unit of rhythm in English poetry is the *foot*. A *foot* consists of two, three, or four syllables, one, and only one, of which is accented. Accented syllables are usually marked ╱ ; unaccented, ◡ . The feet commonly used in English verse are the following:

Two-Syllable Feet

Iambus (◡╱). The name "iambus" comes from the Greek word meaning *to assail*. EXAMPLES: assail, revoke, presume. In English verse, in which stress is so important, the term *rising stress* (or *inflection*) is often used to describe a foot with the accent on the final syllable.

Trochee (╱◡). The name "trochee," which means *running*, illustrates the foot. EXAMPLES: broken, treasure, morning. The term *falling stress* (or *inflection*) is often used to describe a foot with the accent on the first syllable.

Three-Syllable Feet

Anapæst (◡◡╱). "Anapæst" in Greek means *struck back*.
Examples: indi͜sti͝nct, i͜ncomplete. This is *rising* stress.

Dactyl (╱◡◡). "Dactyl," derived from the Greek word for *finger*, with its one long and two short joints, is the reverse of anapæst. Examples: wilderness, murmuring, beautiful. This is *falling* stress.

Four-Syllable Foot

Pæon (╱◡◡◡), (◡◡◡╱). "Pæon" is derived from the Greek word for a song of joy. Examples: exquisitely, aquamarine. The stress may then be either *rising* or *falling*.

Unusual Feet

Two other feet are said to occur sometimes in English poetry: the spondee (— —), derived from the Greek word *to pour out*, used in hymns accompanying libations, and the pyrrhic (◡◡). Both feet have two syllables of about equal length; in the spondee they are long and in the pyrrhic they are short. Since in English one syllable is almost always slightly accented, for all practical purposes these feet become iambic or trochaic.

METER

The *meter*, or measure, of a line of poetry is determined by the kind of foot used and by the number of feet in the line. This number may vary from one to eight, as follows:

1 foot (*monometer*). Examples found in "Work," by Angela Morgan (p. 117).

2 feet (*dimeter*) Examples found in "Nature's Friend," by William H. Davies (p. 212).

3 feet (*trimeter*). Examples found in "Cotswold Love," by John Drinkwater (p. 171).

4 feet (*tetrameter*). Examples found in "Trees," by Joyce Kilmer (p. 222).

5 feet (*pentameter*). Examples found in "The Great Lover," by Rupert Brooke (p. 151).

6 feet (*hexameter*). Examples found in "The Dawn Wind," by Rudyard Kipling (p. 209).

7 feet (*heptameter*). Examples found in "The Voice of Christmas," by Harry Kemp (p. 242).

8 feet (*octameter*). No example in this collection.

The line, from "The Soldier," by Rupert Brooke (p. 14),

$$\breve{\cup} \;\prime \quad \breve{\cup} \quad \prime \quad \breve{\cup} \quad \cup \quad \prime \quad \breve{\cup} \quad \prime$$
If I | should die, | think on|ly this | of me

is called iambic pentameter (written 5 ∪ ′).

The line, from "Kilmeny," by Alfred Noyes (p. 25),

$$\cup \quad \cup \quad \prime \quad \cup \quad \cup \quad \prime \quad \cup \quad \cup \quad \prime \quad \cup \quad \cup \quad \prime$$
It was dark | when Kilmen|y came home | from her quest

is called anapæstic tetrameter (4 ∪ ∪ ′).

The line, from "The Barrel-Organ," by Alfred Noyes,

$$\cup \quad \cup \quad \prime \quad \cup \cup \cup \quad \prime \cup \cup \cup \quad \prime \quad \cup \quad \cup \quad \cup \quad \prime$$
There's a | barrel-organ | carolling a | cross a golden | street

is pæonic tetrameter with two extra unaccented syllables at the beginning and an incomplete last foot (4 ′ ∪ ∪ ∪).

MUSICAL NOTATION OF POETRY

Another method of indicating the meter of poetry is by music notes. In this method the unit of time is the eighth note, or quaver (♪). An iambic foot, for example, would be represented as an eighth followed by a stressed quarter, or ♪ ♩ . In musical notation the bar comes before the accented beat instead of marking the end of the foot. The musical notation of an iambic tetrameter line is

I |think that | I shall | never | see

JOYCE KILMER, "Trees" (p 222)

A line in pæonic tetrameter would be written as follows:

There's a | barrel-organ | carolling a | cross a golden | street.

ALFRED NOYES, "The Barrel-Organ"

VARIATIONS IN RHYTHM

Verse that did not vary in rhythm, that followed an identical pattern of accented and unaccented syllables line after line, would soon become as monotonous as the beating of a tom-tom. Much of the music of any poem depends on the poet's skillful use of devices to introduce variety into the metrical pattern, while retaining the rhythm of the poem as a whole. Among these devices are the following:

PAUSES WITHIN THE LINE

Often an unaccented syllable is omitted, and a pause supplies its place. This pause, like the *rest* in music, is used for emphasis.

Whispering | always, | "Rest, ∧ | rest." ∧

SARA TEASDALE, "The Cloud" (p. 206)

A pause may occur with no omission of syllables within a long line of poetry. It is used constantly in a line of more than ten syllables. This rhythmical pause is called a *cæsura* (marked thus, ||). It usually comes at the close of a phrase or thought, and the shifting, from line to line, of the point at which it occurs is one effective means of giving variety and rhythmic beauty to the verse.

This variation in position is shown in the following lines:

So it's home again, || and home again, || America for me!
My heart is turning home again, || and there I long to be,
In the land of youth and freedom || beyond the ocean bars,
Where the air is full of sunlight || and the flag is full of stars.

HENRY VAN DYKE, "Home Thoughts from Europe" (p. 10)

SUBSTITUTION OF FEET

Frequently feet of rising stress, iambic and anapæstic, are substituted for each other; likewise feet of falling stress, trochaic and dactylic. For example, in the following iambic line, the fifth, sixth, and seventh feet are anapæstic.

ᵕ ′ | ᵕ ′ | ᵕᵕ ′ | ᵕ ′ | ᵕᵕ ′ | ᵕ ′ | ᵕᵕ ′
And he | has found | eter|nal peace | *in the light* | of his Heav|en'y Star.

DUNCAN TOVEY, "The Last Pilot" (p. 26)

Often in an iambic line a trochee is substituted for the first foot or for the foot immediately following the cæsural pause.

′ ᵕ | ᵕ ′ | ᵕ ′ | ᵕ ′ | ᵕ ′
This is | the day | my dear|est child | was born.

LLOYD MIFFLIN, "April Speaks" (p. 195)

′ ᵕ | ᵕ ′ | ′ ᵕ | ᵕ ′ | ᵕ ′
Land of | our hope, || *land of* | the sing|ing stars.

ALFRED NOYES, "Princeton" (p. 9)

VARIATION IN THE NUMBER OF SYLLABLES

Extra unaccented syllables that do not belong in the regular verse scheme frequently come at the beginning or the end of a line or after a cæsural pause.

ᵕ ′ | ᵕ ′ | ᵕ ′ | ᵕ ′ | ᵕ ′ | ᵕ ′ | ᵕ ′ | ᵕ ′ ᵕ
For ev'|ry war|bler in | the wood | a song | of joy | was hum|*ming.*

DOUGLAS MALLOCH, "June" (p. 201)

Frequently, too, an unaccented syllable or syllables are cut from the beginning or the end of a line. Illustrations follow.

′ ᵕ | ′ ᵕ | ′ ᵕ | ᵕ ᵕ | ′ ᵕ
There's a | far high | trail where the | pines are,
′ ᵕ | ′ ᵕ | ′ ᵕ ᵕ | ′
There's a | gray faint | trail to the | dawn, ∧
′ ᵕ | ′ ᵕ | ′ ᵕ ᵕ | ′ ᵕ
There's a | sudden | hush on the | hillside—
′ ᵕ | ′ ′ | ′
Look! the | last star's | gone! ∧

MARY CAROLYN DAVIES, "The Peak" (p. 251)

RHYME

Rhyme is the use of similar sounds at the close of lines or half-lines in order to bind them together. It makes use of accented syllables and is subject to three cardinal rules:

1. The vowel sounds of the rhymed words must be alike; as *fair* and *compare*.

2. The sounds before the vowels must differ; as *f* and *p* in *fair* and *compare*.

3. The sounds after the vowels, if any, must be identical; as *morn* and *forlorn*. If the lines end with unaccented syllables, these syllables must be identical; as *ringing* and *winging*.

Rhymes which are confined to single accented syllables are called masculine, as *field* and *concealed*. Double rhymes, or those with final identical unaccented syllables, like *merry* and *very*, are called feminine. Feminine rhymes imply a more emotional quality and call for a softer enunciation of the closing phrases. The use of terminal feminine rhymes alternating with masculine is shown in "Heroes," by Laurence Housman (p. 12).

The occurrence of rhyming words within the line at the end of each half-verse is called *internal rhyme*. Its use adds melody to the line. It is used freely in Oxenham's "Where Are You Going, Great-Heart?" (p. 227).

> "With your eager *face* and your fiery *grace*."
> "To fight a *fight* with all my *might*."

Internal rhyme with feminine ending is used in the line

> When the soul is just *awaking* like a lily blossom *breaking*.

> DENIS A. McCARTHY, "Ah, Sweet is Tipperary" (p. 197)

Alliteration is sometimes called *initial rhyme*. It is the systematic repetition of the initial sound in two or more words in close succession. In early times it was the structural element in English poetry. In this formal use one accented syllable, or both, in the first half of the line and one in the second had the same initial sound.

*W*renching the *r*afters from their ancient *r*est,
He held the *r*idgepole up.

EDWIN MARKHAM, "Lincoln, the Man of the People" (p. 185)

Alliteration may now occur anywhere in a line or in successive lines.

The friendly *w*elcome of the *w*ayside *w*ell.

EDWIN MARKHAM, "Lincoln, the Man of the People" (p. 185)

BLANK VERSE

Blank verse is unrhymed iambic pentameter ($\smile$). It holds a very important place in English verse, being well suited to epics, dramas, and long narrative poems, such as Milton's "Paradise Lost," Shakespeare's plays, and Tennyson's "Idylls of the King."

In English blank verse the pause, or cæsura, is not restricted to the middle of the line. As its position depends on the thought of the line, it may occur after or in any foot. This free placement of the cæsura and the use of the "run on," or unstopped, line, in which there is no sense pause at the end, give unusual flexibility to this form of verse. Different poems in blank verse may be appreciably different in rhythmic movement. Poems in blank verse in this collection include "A Birthnight Candle," by John Finley (p. 58); "Dawn in the Desert," by Clinton Scollard (p. 210); "Lincoln, the Man of the People," by Edwin Markham (p. 184).

STANZA FORMS

A stanza is a group of two or more consecutive lines bound together by end rhyme. The form of the stanza is determined by the emotional content of the poem, but each stanza, even if "run on," conveys one definite impression. A stanza is the largest measure of subdivision in a poem. When the stanzaic structure is regular each stanza has the same number of lines, the same rhyme scheme, and the same meter. Blank verse has no stanzas.

In indicating stanza structure letters are used to represent the rhyme scheme. Thus, *a b a b* means a four-line stanza with alternate rhyme.

THE TWO-LINE STANZA

A *couplet* is a pair of rhymed verses. Couplets written in iambic tetrameter $(4 \cup \prime)$, and rhyming *a a b b* etc., are called *romantic verse*; couplets in iambic pentameter $(5 \cup \prime)$, and rhyming *a a b b* etc., are called *heroic couplets*.

Romantic verse is illustrated in this collection by A. E. Housman's lyric, "Loveliest of Trees" (p. 221); the heroic couplet is used in "Nature's Miracle," by David Fallon (p. 205). "The Great Lover," by Rupert Brooke (p. 151), illustrates the frequent use of the "unstopped couplet."

Ballad measure is properly iambic heptameter $(7 \cup \prime)$ couplets with constant medial cæsura. An example is Kipling's "The Ballad of East and West" (p. 33), which shows also frequent substitution of anapæsts for the regular iambic foot. Usually in modern poetry each long line of the couplet is divided into two shorter lines of four accents $(4 \cup \prime)$ and three accents $(3 \cup \prime)$ respectively, with alternate rhyme *a b a b* or *a b c b*. This is the *common meter* of the hymnals. It is well illustrated in "Songs for my Mother," by Anna Hempstead Branch (p. 59), and in "To the Bard of Auld Lang Syne," by James Main Dixon (p. 181).

THE THREE-LINE STANZA

A triplet is the simplest form of three-line stanza, all *a a a*. Examples in this collection are "A Consecration," by John Masefield (p. 133), and "The Voice of Christmas," by Harry Kemp (p. 242).

The *terza rima* is a less familiar form, in which the first and third lines rhyme, while the second line gives the rhyme to the first and third lines of the following stanza, as *a b a, b c b, c d c*, etc. An illustration is found in "A Saint's Hours," by Sarah N. Cleghorn (p. 148).

THE FOUR-LINE STANZA, OR QUATRAIN

This is a form familiar in old ballads and many hymns. It is used in a great variety of rhymes and meters. Many forms are illustrated in this collection, including the forms *a a b b* in "The Supreme Sacrifice," by John S. Arkwright (p. 27), and *a b a b* in "Heroes," by Laurence Housman (p. 12).

THE FIVE-LINE STANZA

These examples show some of the variations in the five-line stanza: *a b a a b* in "Song of Life," by Florence E. Coates (p. 234), and *a b c c b* in "A Street Car Miracle," by Minnie L. Upton (p. 139).

THE SIX-LINE STANZA

Many variations are possible in the rhyme scheme of this form. Some of them are *a a b b c c* in "The Cloud," by Sara Teasdale (p. 206); *a b a b c c* in "The Recessional," by Rudyard Kipling (p. 5); *a a a b a b* in "Across the Fields to Anne," by Richard Burton (p. 177); and *a b c b d b* in "The Spires of Oxford," by Winifred Letts (p. 20).

THE SEVEN-LINE STANZA

One of the best-known forms of this stanza is the *a b a b b c c* iambic pentameter form, first used by Chaucer in some of his "Canterbury Tales," and called rhyme royal after James I, who used it in his "King's Quair." It is not illustrated in this collection, but is used in Masefield's "Dauber," "The Daffodil Fields," and "The Widow in the Bye Street."

THE EIGHT-LINE STANZA

The double quatrain and linked quatrains are used in many variations of rhyme and meter. Two of them are *a b a b c d c d* in "Vitai Lampada," by Henry Newbolt (p. 19), and *a b a b c d e d* in "America the Beautiful," by Katharine Lee Bates (p. 3).

One famous form, written in iambic pentameter and rhyming *a b a b a b c c*, is called the *ottava rima*. It is found in Byron's "Don Juan" and in Keats's "Isabella." It is not illustrated in this collection.

THE NINE-LINE STANZA

A Spenserian stanza has eight lines of iambic pentameter and a ninth line of iambic hexameter (an *Alexandrine*). It has the rhyme scheme of the French ballade (p. 268) eight-line stanza (*a b a b b c b c*), with the addition of a ninth line with the *c* rhyme (*a b a b b c b c c*). This ninth line is usually a summarizing line for the stanza. This is the stanza form of Spenser's "Faerie Queene," Keats's "Eve of St. Agnes," and many other well-known poems, but is not illustrated in this collection.

SPECIAL VERSE FORMS

THE SONNET

The *sonnet* is a poem of fourteen lines written in iambic pentameter. There are two types: the Italian, or Petrarchan, form, and the English, or Shakespearean, form.

The Italian form is more strict both in its rhyme scheme and in the thought development. It consists of an octave, composed of two linked quatrains, and a sestet, composed of two linked tercets. The octave presents the problem; the sestet, the solution. The perfect Italian sonnet has two rhymes in the octave, and either two or three, which may vary in arrangement (*c d c d c d, c d d c d c, c d e d c e*, etc.), in the sestet. It may be represented graphically thus:

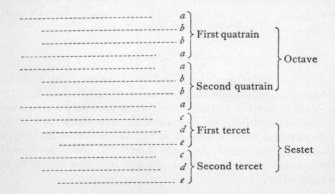

Examples of this strict form are "April Speaks," by Lloyd Mifflin (p. 195), and "As in a Rose-Jar," by Thomas S. Jones, Jr. (p. 240).

A freer treatment of the Italian sonnet frequently seen is illustrated by Rupert Brooke's "The Soldier" (p. 14).

The English sonnet allows greater freedom in arrangement. It consists of three independent quatrains and a concluding couplet. Its form is as follows:

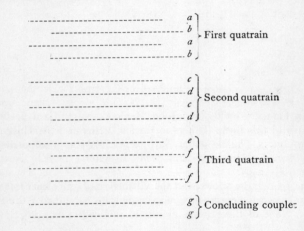

An example of this form is found in "The School Boy reads his Iliad," by David Morton (p. 69).

THE RONDEAU

The *rondeau*, originally a French form, consists of thirteen lines, not including the repeated refrain, divided into three stanzas. The refrain, which is a repetition of the opening phrase of the first line, comes in at the close of the second stanza and is repeated at the close of the third. This refrain gives the keynote of the poem. The rondeau has only two rhyme sounds and the refrain (represented by *R*).

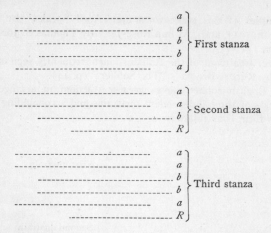

"In Flanders Fields," by John McCrae (p. 15), is a perfect example of this form. Others in this collection are "At Husking Time," by E. Pauline Johnson (p. 203); "With Strawberries," by William E. Henley (p. 201); and "In After Days," by Austin Dobson (p. 246).

The rondel, the triolet, and the villanelle are other fixed forms whose charm is dependent upon the delicate handling of the refrain. None of these forms appear in this collection.

THE BALLADE

The *ballade*, also of French origin, has two fixed forms. That most commonly met in English poetry consists of three stanzas of eight lines each, followed by a quatrain called the envoy, or message. Each of the stanzas and the envoy close with the same refrain, which is the characteristic feature of a ballade. The number of feet in the line is not determined; usually the ballade is written in trimeter or tetrameter. The rhyme scheme is difficult, inasmuch as the same rhymes must be used throughout. It usually is *a b a b b c b c*, or two linked quatrains for the stanzas, and *b c b c* for the envoy.

Examples of this form are "A Ballad of Heroes," by Austin Dobson (p. 11), and "Ballade by the Fire," by Edwin A. Robinson (p. 235).

Vers Libre, or Free Verse

In addition to the poetic forms already discussed, there has been revived within the present century a type of poetry in which regular rhythm and rhyme are disregarded. This form, found in the Bible and in poems by Walt Whitman and others, is now called *vers libre* or *free verse*. It is a protest against the regularity and uniformity of earlier forms. In place of rhyme and a regular meter, free verse depends on the grouping, or phrasing, of a varying number of stressed and unstressed syllables, repeated at irregular intervals. According to the Imagist poets, Imagism, one school of free verse, has three very simple cardinal rules. The poet should always study to treat directly the subject chosen for his theme. He should use no word which does not contribute directly to this vivid presentation. The musical phrase, not the metrical foot, should be made the basis of rhythm. "These principles," they say, "are not new; they have fallen into desuetude. They are the essentials of all great poetry, indeed of all great literature." It is therefore not a mere change in the form of poetry, but a changed point of view, which the Imagist poets represent.

Miss Amy Lowell, one of the foremost exponents of vers libre in America, gives six rules for writing it. In condensed form these rules are as follows:

1. Use the language of common speech, but employ always the exact word, not the merely decorative word.

2. Create new rhythms, as expressive of new moods, and give up copying old rhythms which merely echo old moods.

3. Claim absolute freedom in the choice of the subject.

4. Always present an image.

5. Strive to produce poetry that is hard and clear, never blurred and indefinite.

6. Study concentration.

A list of books and articles which discuss the subject of free verse extensively is included in the bibliographies on page 303.

Some of the poems written in free verse in this collection are "Patterns," by Amy Lowell (p. 49); "On the Palisades," by Louis Untermeyer (p. 159); "Monotone," by Carl Sandburg (p. 208); "Squall," by Leonora Speyer (p. 206).

KINDS OF LYRIC POETRY

Lyric poetry, which is the most melodious, the most songlike, of all forms of poetry, expresses personal emotion, either real or imagined. It is to poetry what the informal, personal essay is to prose—a bit of life seen through the eyes of the author. Thus a lyric may deal with practically any phase of life—love of country, love of man or woman, love of nature, celebration of an event, or the setting forth of those high ideals toward which mankind is always striving.

Certain lyrics portraying definite moods have come to have fixed conventions. It is therefore convenient to know the names of these different kinds of lyrics, and the moods for which they stand.

THE ELEGY

The *elegy*, a dignified, reflective lyric, laments a real or an imagined loss by death. "Heroes," by Laurence Housman (p. 12), is one of the best recent elegies.

THE SONG

Songs, or verse intended to be sung, such as love songs, patriotic songs, and hymns, are simple, brief, and direct in expression, whether they arise from personal or from group emotions. In this collection are many lyrics well known for their musical settings. Among them are "America the Beautiful," by Katharine Lee Bates (p. 3); "Duna," by Marjorie L. C. Pickthall (p. 173); "The Supreme Sacrifice," by John S. Arkwright (p. 27).

The Ode

The *ode* is written in celebration of some person, event, or abstract feeling, and is characterized by exaltation of feeling and elevation of style. It is the most involved form of English verse. The Greek, or Pindaric, ode, which was primarily used for chanting in chorus, is divided into three parts, the strophe, antistrophe, and epode, each with its own intricate rhyme scheme and meter. The English, or irregular, ode shows great variety in versification and much individual freedom in the arrangement of its stanzas and its verse lengths.

This collection includes no elaborate ode. Gray's "The Progress of Poesy" is one of the best examples in English of the Pindaric ode; Wordsworth's Ode on "Intimations of Immortality," of the English form. A very simple form is found in John Buchan's "In Praise of the Royal Scots Fusiliers" (p. 21).

For a more comprehensive study of the form of English poetry the following books are valuable:

ALDEN, RAYMOND M. English Verse. Henry Holt and Company.

BRIGHT and MILLER. The Elements of English Versification. Ginn and Company.

GAYLEY, YOUNG, and KURTZ. English Poetry: Its Principles and Progress. The Macmillan Company.

GUMMERE, F. B. Handbook of Poetics. Ginn and Company.

MATTHEWS, BRANDER. A Study of Versification. Houghton Mifflin Company.

NEILSON, WILLIAM ALLAN. The Essentials of Poetry. Houghton Mifflin Company.

PERRY, BLISS. A Study of Poetry. Houghton Mifflin Company.

THE ENJOYMENT OF POETRY

(Suggestions for the Teacher)

The awakening of a love of poetry and the upbuilding of the power of enjoying it require a careful approach to the study of the author's thought and his skill in expressing it. With younger readers this approach may well be made through a preliminary discussion of the marked interest in present-day poetry, the number of contemporary writers of good verse, the amount and the quality of the verse inspired by the World War (especially in the minor writers), and the recent successful achievement of magazines devoted solely to verse, as well as the attention given to poetry in many types of current magazines and in the newspapers.

Poetic interest and enjoyment may be furthered by the reading aloud of some of the more familiar of these recent poems so that the music may help the thought to bring about a gradual discovery of the variety of pleasure which poetry gives. Students may be encouraged to find verse which appeals to them in newspapers, magazines, and collections of poetry, and to read these poems to their classmates, justifying and upholding their choice. By beginning with the simpler, more obvious poems, the pupil will develop an appreciation of the more complex and imaginative verse, until the Poet stands disclosed as the Seer, who sees and reveals the truth and beauty of life ; as the Painter, who depicts in strong, beautiful, and imperishable words the thoughts which help to mold the race ; and as the Musician, who in purposeful swing and rhyme sings strains of undying melody.

To aid in securing this progress toward poetic enjoyment, a study plan which is adaptable to the poems in this collection is given. This plan is of course only suggestive. It is hoped that it may help the teacher to new points of view or to different ways of approaching the study of a poem. It is hardly necessary to say that to give this plan of study to the pupils for home work or to use it as a whole with one poem after another would deaden the study of poetry and thus defeat the purpose for which the outline was intended.

GENERAL PLAN FOR THE STUDY OF A POEM

I. The *thought* of the poem.

1. What has the author said? Restate this in a sentence or two in your own words.
    a. Through whose eyes or from what viewpoint does the poet see his theme?
    b. How has he expressed his mood?
        (1) Is his treatment of his subject realistic, imaginative, serious, playful, or humorous?
        (2) Has he made use of any such devices as conversation, monologue, or allegory to express his theme?
    c. Has he drawn upon legend, myth, or art, or recreated a tradition to express his theme?

2. What is the message of the poem?
    a. Does it present a new, an unusual, or an unfamiliar thought?
    b. Does it present a familiar thought in a new or beautiful way?
    c. Does it portray affection for the familiar things of daily life,—determination, pride, patriotism, high hope, faith, courage, joy, intense realization of beauty, or any other worthy feelings,—or does it immortalize any worthy action?
    d. Does it kindle your imagination, or awaken new ambitions, hopes, or purposes?
    e. Does it stimulate to better living?

3. Why was the poem written?
    a. For the thoughts it contains?
    b. For the pictures it portrays?
    c. For the ideas it suggests?
    d. What is its strongest appeal?

4. Who would enjoy it most?
  a. To what type or age of people does it appeal?
    (1) To children? To men or women?
    (2) To all people of all races and ages?
  b. What kind of enjoyment does it bring?
    (1) Is it most impressive for its theme?
    (2) Is it most memorable for its word pictures?
    (3) Is its melody especially haunting and unforgettable?
5. What line or lines give the keynote of the poem?
  a. Has any other writer, either past or present, made similar use of this theme?
  b. How does the treatment of this theme vary with the different writers?
  c. What is distinctive in the treatment of this theme in this poem?

II. The *expression* of the poem.
  1. What is worthy in the language of the poem?
    a. Is it especially noticeable for simplicity of diction?
    b. Does the wording make the pictures clear and graphic?
    c. What vivid words are used to suggest action, color, sound, odor, or taste?
    d. What words or groups of words are used which are especially expressive of the thought — picturesque, melodious, or rich in association?
    e. Is any symbolic language used? Do the symbols indicate any especial mood or attitude of mind?
  2. Is there any evident repetition of letters, or sounds, or words?
    a. Where are these repetitions found?
    b. What is the effect of these repetitions?
  3. Are the comparisons set forth forcefully and vitally?
  4. If characters are represented, how are they portrayed? Does the character portrayal in verse differ from that in the novel or the short story?
  5. What do the pictures, or sounds, or poetic language add to your pleasure or understanding of the poem?
  6. What is the most memorable line in the poem?

III. The *form* of the poem.

   1. In what structural form is the poem arranged?

      a. Are there stanzas? If so, are the stanzas and the lines in each stanza of the same length?

      b. If no stanzas are used, is there any division within the poem?

      c. What is the thought in each stanza or block of the poem?

      d. What poems of similar poetic structure do you know?

      e. What determines a poet's use of any structural form?

   2. Is rhyme used?

      a. If so, how regularly and how often is it used?

      b. Is there internal as well as end rhyme?

      c. What effect is gained by this use of rhyme?

   3. Is the rhythm particularly noticeable?

      a. What is its "march" time?

      b. Is it suited to the emotions expressed in the poem?

      c. Does it reflect or intensify the author's mood?

      d. Does the rhythm or the wording suggest any musical instrument or musical composition?

      e. What is the best line (or lines) for language or sound?

      f. Is the singing quality of the poet especially evident?

   4. Have the details been well selected and well arranged so that the poem records a definite impression?

IV. *Creative reaction.*

   1. Can you imitate the verse form of this poem by writing a summary or a brief appreciation of it?

   2. Can you expand an idea suggested by some word or thought in this poem into a short original poem?

   3. Can you express some of your own ideas on this theme or a similar one in poetic prose?

   4. Can you rewrite your poetic prose in verse form, paying attention to both thought and meter?

BIOGRAPHICAL NOTES

[All authors, unless otherwise noted, are American by birth.]

ADAMS, JAMES BARTON

Has written occasional poems. The events of his life are unknown.

ARKWRIGHT, JOHN STANHOPE (1872–   )

English lawyer and member of Parliament. Author of "The Last Muster" and "The Supreme Sacrifice and Other Poems."
"The Supreme Sacrifice" is considered the finest hymn produced by the World War. It was sung at the interment of the Unknown Soldier at Arlington Cemetery on Armistice Day, 1921.

AUSLANDER, JOSEPH (1897–   )

Born in Philadelphia; educated at Harvard, where he is now an instructor in the Department of English. His poems are appearing in the *Atlantic Monthly* and other magazines.

AUSTIN, ALFRED (1835–1913)

English lawyer; later a successful London journalist. Poet laureate from 1896 to 1913, succeeding Lord Tennyson. Author of several volumes of light prose, poetic dramas, and much lyric and patriotic verse.

BAKER, KARLE WILSON (Mrs. Thomas E. Baker) (1878–   )

A Southern writer of stories, essays, poems, and contributor to magazines. Born in Arkansas; now living in Texas. Her early work appeared under the pen name "Charlotte Wilson." Her verse is collected in a recent volume, "Blue Smoke."

BASHFORD, HERBERT (1871–   )

Journalist and author; formerly state librarian of Washington; until recently on the editorial staff of the *San Francisco Chronicle*. Writer of dramas, stories, and verse, and contributor to leading magazines.

BATES, KATHARINE LEE (1859–   )

Professor of English at Wellesley College since 1891. Author, lecturer, translator, editor, and poet. Has published many books of travel, stories, and poems for children. "America the Beautiful" is her best-known volume of verse; "Yellow Clover" (1922) is her latest.

BENÉT, WILLIAM ROSE (1886–   )

Poet, essayist, novelist, and critic. Began as a free-lance writer. Was assistant editor of the *Century Magazine* when he entered the air service as second lieutenant. Now associate editor of the "Literary Review" of the *New York Evening Post*. Has published five volumes of poems and humorous verse; the two latest are "Burglars of the Zodiac" and "Moons of Grandeur."

BINYON, LAURENCE (1869–   )

English poet and dramatist. A cousin of Stephen Phillips. Born in Lancaster; educated at St. Paul's School and Oxford University. Has been in the Department of Printed Books at the British Museum since 1893; is now Assistant Keeper of Oriental Prints and Drawings. Author of several books, including "Poetry and Modern Life" and "The Secret" (1920).

BOURDILLON, FRANCIS WILLIAM (1852–1921)

English writer, educator, translator, and editor. Educated at Oxford; became the private resident tutor of the sons of Prince and Princess Christian of Denmark. Author of several volumes of poems. His best-known poem, "The Night hath a Thousand Eyes," is familiar also as a song.

BRADLEY, WILLIAM ASPENWALL (1878–   )

Author, critic, editor, writer on art topics, and designer. Connected with the Yale University Press and many magazines. Served during the war as first lieutenant in the Sanitary Corps, A.E.F. One of his best-known books of verse is "Garlands and Wayfarings."

BRALEY, BERTON (1882–   )

Contributor of poems and many short stories to leading magazines and newspapers. Was a reporter on Western and New York papers and during the war served as special correspondent in northern Europe. "Buddy Ballads" and "Songs of the Workaday World" are the best known of his four books of verse. His latest publication is a novel, "The Sheriff of Silver Bow."

BRANCH, ANNA HEMPSTEAD

New England writer. Contributor in prose and verse to leading magazines. Her lyric poetry and dramas, published in "The Heart of the Road," "The Shoes that Danced," and "Rose of the Wind," are marked by rare imaginative quality and beauty.

BRIDGES, ROBERT (1844–   )

Present English poet laureate, succeeding Alfred Austin in 1913. Began his career as a physician, and practiced until 1882. A traveler, musician, and scholar, he has lived an unhurried, meditative life. One of the founders of the S. P. E. (Society for Pure English). Writes plays, essays, and masques, nearly all classical in theme and treatment. Holds for the year 1923–1924 the fellowship of creative literature (held in 1922–1923 by Robert Frost) at the University of Michigan.

BROOKE, RUPERT (1887–1915)

One of the most brilliant of the younger Georgian poets. Son of the Assistant Headmaster of Rugby. At Rugby and Cambridge he excelled in athletics. His "Letters from America" gives his experiences in the United States and Canada when on his way to the South Seas. Enlisted as soon as Great Britain declared war; served in Belgium and the Dardanelles campaign. Died while in service in the Ægean, and was buried on the island of Skyros. An interesting account of his buoyant life is published in his "Collected Poems." He has been described as "strong, vivid, fearless, and versatile, a golden young Apollo."

BROWN, ABBIE FARWELL

A life-long resident of Boston. Author of many short stories, plays, songs, cantatas, stories for children, and verse, including "Fresh Posies" and "Songs of Sixpence."

BUCHAN, JOHN (1875–   )

Novelist, war correspondent, critic, and historian. A native of Peeblesshire in Scotland. Educated at Glasgow University and Oxford, where he won the Newdigate Prize. His publications include "Prester John," "The Marquis of Montrose," "Greenmantle," "The Path of the King," "Poems Scots and English," and "The History of the Great War." He has edited Nelson's "History of the War" (24 vols., 1915–1919) and "Nations of Today."

BURNET, DANA (1888–   )

Journalist, and author of many novels, short stories, and of poetry, which is now collected in the volume "Gayheart." Was on the staff of the New York Sun for seven years, served as special writer in France in 1917–1918. Has recently published a novel, "The Lack" (1921). He now lives in Ogunquit, Maine.

BURR, AMELIA JOSEPHINE (Mrs. Carl H. Elmore) (1878–)

A New Jersey author who follows literature as a profession. Writes plays, novels, and verse, especially ballads. "Hearts Awake" and "Little Houses" are her latest volumes.

BURTON, RICHARD (1861–)

Professor of English literature at the University of Minnesota. Author of many essays, biographies, books of criticism, and lyrics. Widely known as a lecturer, critic of the drama, and for his books on plays and playwrights. His verse includes "Dumb in June," "Lyrics of Brotherhood," and "Message and Melody."

CAMPBELL, NANCY (Mrs. Joseph Campbell)

Irish writer of folk tales; among them is "The Little People." Her husband, the Irish poet and dramatist, illustrated her "Agnus Dei."

CARMAN, (WILLIAM) BLISS (1861–)

Canadian by birth, but has lived in the United States for many years. Was on the editorial staff of New York and Chicago papers. Poet and journalist. Collaborated with Richard Hovey in "Songs from Vagabondia." Has produced many volumes of poetry, including "The Green Book of the Bards" and "Pipes of Pan." His latest book is "April Airs." Was recently crowned as Canada's major poet by the Canadian Authors' Association.

CARRUTH, WILLIAM HERBERT (1859–)

A native of Kansas, and for twenty-six years professor in the University of Kansas. Professor of comparative literature and head of the English department at Stanford University since 1913. Author of prose and verse, editor, translator, and contributor to philological publications.

CARRYL, GUY WETMORE (1873–1904)

Born in New York, the son of Charles Edward Carryl, also a gifted writer. Journalist, foreign correspondent for magazines and publications, and writer of light verse, brilliant in rhyme. Best known for his burlesques of the nursery rhymes: "Mother Goose for Grown Ups," "Fables for the Frivolous," and "Grimm Tales made Gay."

CAWEIN, MADISON (1865–1914)

A Southern poet and author of many volumes of verse. His descriptions of nature are exceptionally accurate, for Cawein was a "comrade of nature," possessed of a naturalist's careful observation and eagerness for truth. He has been called "the Keats of Kentucky."

CHENEY, JOHN VANCE (1848–1922)

Author, editor, and writer of essays and poems. Was public librarian in San Francisco, and later in Chicago. The latest of his seven books of verse is called "At the Silver Gate."

CHESTERTON, GILBERT KEITH (1874–   )

Born in Kensington, London. Began reviewing art books for the *Bookman*, and since then has been active as a journalist, essayist, novelist, critic, historian, parodist, lecturer, and poet. Contributes plays, stories, and verse to leading magazines.

"Lepanto," with its rhythmic beat and march time, is considered one of the finest of modern chants.

CLEGHORN, SARAH NORCLIFFE (1876–   )

Novelist and poet, very familiar with life in Vermont. Has collaborated with Dorothy Canfield Fisher. Her collected verse is found in "Portraits and Protests."

CLOVER, SAMUEL TRAVERS (1859–   )

Newspaper writer and editor. Born in London, England. Began his newspaper career in 1880 by making a trip round the world. Was a reporter on Western and Chicago papers, and a staff reporter during several Indian uprisings. Has edited papers in Chicago, Richmond, and Los Angeles. Author of several novels, sketches, stories, and poems of Western life.

COATES, FLORENCE EARLE (Mrs. Edward H. Coates) (1850–   )

Contributor of many lyrics to leading American magazines. Was unanimously elected poet laureate of Pennsylvania by the State Federation of Women's Clubs. Has published several volumes of verse, including "The Unconquered Air" and "Pro Patria."

CONE, HELEN GRAY (1859–   )

Professor of English at Hunter College, New York. Author of several volumes of verse, her latest being "The Coat without a Seam."

COOLBRITH, INA DONNA (1844–   )

Western poet and contributor to magazines. Was public librarian in Oakland and San Francisco. Was associated with Bret Harte while he was editor of the *Overland Monthly*. "Songs from the Golden Gate" is the best known of her three books of verse. Has been created poet laureate of California by the governor and legislature of that state.

COOPER, JAMES FENIMORE, JR. (1892–1918)

Great-grandson of James Fenimore Cooper, the novelist. A captain in the A. E. F., he was the first member of the class of 1913 of Yale to die in service. His poems, first issued in college publications, are now collected in a memorial volume, "Afterglow."

CRAFTON, ALLEN (1890–   )

A young poet of varied life experiences. Born in Illinois. Has been a street-car motorman, a director of a Little Theater, an aviator in the army, and is now professor of Dramatic Art at Kansas University. Author of two plays, "The Stranger Star," a fantasy, and poems published in various magazines.

CRAWFORD, CHARLOTTE HOLMES

A resident of New York. Occasional contributor of verse to various magazines.

DALY, JOHN (1888–   )

Dramatic editor of the *Washington Post*. Served in the A. E. F. His "Toast to the Flag," with its vigor and original rhyme scheme, had widespread popularity in America during the World War.

DALY, THOMAS AUGUSTINE (1871–   )

Editorial writer, poet, lecturer, and newspaper manager. While he is best known for his half-humorous, half-pathetic dialect poems of Italian and Irish immigrants, his verse is not exclusively in dialect. Was president of the American Press Humorists. Among his more recent publications are "Little Polly's Poems," "Songs of Wedlock," and "McAroni Ballads" (1919).

DAVIES, MARY CAROLYN (Mrs. Leland Davies) (1888–   )

Writer of short stories, plays, and much verse, collected in "Drums in Our Street" and "Youth Riding."

DAVIES, WILLIAM HENRY (1870–   )

Poet and author; born in Montana of Welsh parents. His "Autobiography of a Super-Tramp" describes his life as a tramp in America and England, on cattle ships, as a peddler, and as a street singer of hymns. He was thirty-four years old when his first volume of verse was published. The latest of his eight books of verse is entitled "Forty New Poems." He has recently assumed the editorship of the London *Form*.

DE LA MARE, WALTER JOHN (1873–   )

English poet and novelist, now living in a suburb of London. Was a close personal friend of Rupert Brooke. Widely known for his delightful child verse, character studies, and imaginative lyrics. His fancy and genius are best shown in "Peacock Pie" (1913) and in his novel, "The Memoirs of a Midget." Many of his poems have been set to music. His "Collected Poems" appeared in 1920.

DIXON, JAMES MAIN (1856–   )

A native of the Burns country, and educated at Ayr Academy and Edinburgh and St. Andrews universities. For thirteen years professor in the Imperial University of Japan, and an authority on things Japanese. Now professor of comparative literature in the University of Southern California. Has published a study of Matthew Arnold; "The Spiritual Meaning of Tennyson's 'In Memoriam'"; "English Idioms," a standard work. He is co-author of Grant and Dixon's "Manual of Modern Scots," the authoritative treatise on the language.

DOBSON, HENRY AUSTIN (1840–1921)

English poet and editor. Received his LL.D. from Edinburgh University. Was a Fellow of the Royal Society of Literature. Writer of many biographies, essays, and graceful light verse in a great variety of forms. Especially at home in the quaint forms of Old French poetry, —the rondeau, ballade, and similar forms,—which he was largely instrumental in introducing into modern English verse. His poems are now reissued in his "Collected Verse."

DRINKWATER, JOHN (1882–   )

English poet, essayist, and dramatist. Was a co-founder of the Pilgrim Players, and is at present the theatrical manager of the Birmingham Repertory Theater, which was developed by that company. He is also the editor of "Studies in Poetry." A writer of thoughtful, meditative verse; best known in the United States for his historical play "Abraham Lincoln." Among his recent plays are "Mary Stuart," "Oliver Cromwell," and "Robert E. Lee" (1923).

DRISCOLL, LOUISE (1875–   )

Writer of verse and short stories and lecturer on modern poetry. "The Metal Cheeks," a war poem, received first prize from the *Poetry Magazine* in 1914. "The Garden of the West" is her first volume of verse (1922).

DRUMMOND, WILLIAM HENRY (1854–1907)

Canadian writer. A practicing physician in Montreal. An athlete, fond of outdoor life, he became familiar with rural French-Canadian life, which is vividly depicted in his writings. Read and lectured in the United States and Canada. Author of several volumes, one in verse, "The Voyageur."

EDGETT, EDWIN FRANCIS (1867–)

Journalist and newspaper correspondent. Was the dramatic editor of the *Boston Transcript*, and is now its literary editor. Author of books on the drama and many translations from the Japanese.

FALLON, DAVID (1886–)

Captain in the British and Australian forces; now a resident of California. Born in Ireland, trained in India, Africa, and Australia. Awarded the Military Cross for his services as a scout during the World War. Author of "The Big Fight," a stirring account of his varied experiences in the militia, airplane, and tank service in Gallipoli, France, and Belgium.

FINLEY, JOHN HUSTON (1863–)

Widely known as an educational expert. A lecturer, author, contributor to reviews; active in all educational work. In 1917 he was sent to France on a special educational mission. Until 1921 he was president of the University of the State of New York. Is now associate editor of the *New York Times*.

FLECKER, JAMES ELROY (1884–1915)

Young British writer of great originality and poetic gifts. Went to Constantinople and Smyrna on consular service. Loved the East for its picturesqueness and age-old civilization. Married an Athenian. Tuberculosis soon compelled him to remove to Switzerland, where he died. Published verse, essays, and short stories, and left two plays in manuscript.

FOSS, SAM WALTER (1858–1911)

New England newspaper man, editor, lecturer, and reader of his own poems. Was editorial writer for the *Boston Globe* for several years, and later the librarian of the Somerville (Massachusetts) Public Library. The most popular of his five books of poems are "Dreams in Homespun" and "Songs of the Average Man."

FOSTER, JEANNE ROBERT (Mrs. Matlack Foster) (1884–   )

Newspaper writer; now literary editor of the *Review of Reviews*. Her verse includes "Wild Apples," "Neighbors of Yesterday" (narrative poems of the Adirondacks), and "Rock-Flowers."

FRANK FLORENCE KIPER (Mrs. Jerome N. Frank)

Writer of verse and plays. Now living in Chicago. Author of "The Jew to Jesus and Other Poems" and "Cinderelline," a poetical play for children.

FROST, ROBERT (1875–   )

A poet, writing especially of New England farm life. Born in San Francisco. When ten years old he moved to New England, where eight generations of his forefathers had lived. Engaged in farming for several years, taught school, was professor of English at Amherst College, held the fellowship of creative literature at the University of Michigan, and has now returned to Amherst. Author of "A Boy's Will," "North of Boston," "Mountain Interval," and "New Hampshire" (1923) books of strong verse.

GALBRAITH, WILLIAM CAMPBELL (1870–   )

Born at Campbelltown on the Clyde in Scotland. Lieutenant colonel in the British army and C. M. G. (Commander of St. Michael and St. George). Was mentioned four times in dispatches during the World War. His publications include "Highland Heather and Other Songs" and "Soldier Songs from Picardy."

GARLAND, HAMLIN (1860–   )

Well-known novelist, dramatist, writer of many short stories, and several biographies. Is now living in New York. Has published many novels dealing with Western life in America. His lyrics are found in "Prairie Songs."

GIBSON, WILFRID WILSON (1878–   )

English poet, now living in Gloucestershire. Author of almost a dozen books of verse. Served as a private in the World War. For a time he lived in East End, the slum district of London, an experience reflected in his poetry. He has been called the poet of contemporary industrial life because he sets forth in condensed narrative the trials and hopes of common humanity in poems vivid, intense, and compelling. Among his best-known volumes are "Daily Bread," "Fires," "Home," and "Neighbors" (1920).

GIFFORD, FANNIE STEARNS DAVIS (Mrs. Augustus M. Gifford) (1884–)

Contributor of verse and prose to many magazines. Was a teacher of English in Wisconsin; now living in Pittsfield, Massachusetts. Her verse includes "Myself and I" and "Crack o' Dawn." She is a younger sister of William S. Davis, professor of history at the University of Minnesota and author of several historical novels, including "A Friend of Cæsar." Her latest volume (1923) is "The Ancient Beautiful Things."

GILDER, RICHARD WATSON (1844–1909)

Well-known editor of several publications, including *Scribner's Magazine* and the *Century Magazine*. For many years he exercised a potent influence in shaping American periodicals. Author of several biographies, and of many volumes of lyrics, now compiled in his "Collected Verse."

GORE-BOOTH, EVA (1872–)

Irish author; now residing in London. Writer of dramatic poems based on Irish legends. Noteworthy for her mystic, haunting lyrics. Her latest volume is "Broken Glory"; her most characteristic, "The One and the Many."

GOULD, GERALD (1885–)

English journalist; now assistant editor of the *London Daily Herald*. Author of several books of lyrics, essays, and reviews for the weekly and monthly press.

GRAY, AGNES KENDRICK (1894–)

Writer of lyric poetry, appearing in papers and magazines. Now living in New York. "River Dusk and Other Poems" (1923) is her first volume.

GREENE, SARAH PRATT McLEAN (Mrs. Franklin L. Greene) (1856–)

Mrs. Greene has published several novels and volumes of short stories, dealing mainly with New England life, especially among Cape Cod fishermen.

GUEST, EDGAR A. (1881–)

Press humorist. Connected since 1895 with the *Detroit Free Press*; now conducts its column of verse and humorous sketches. Has published much newspaper verse, all definitely appealing to the average reader. He has been called "The People's Poet." "Just Folks" and "Over Here" are his best-known books of verse. His latest volumes are "All That Matters" (1922) and "The Passing Throng" (1923).

GUINEY, LOUISE IMOGEN (1861–1920)

An American writer who devoted her life to literature. Resided in Oxford, England, during the last nineteen years of her life. Published translations, essays of criticism, stories, and poetry characterized by mystic beauty and spiritual valor.

GUITERMAN, ARTHUR (1871–   )

Born of American parentage at Vienna, Austria. Educated at the College of the City of New York. Author of ballads and lyric verse. Lecturer on magazine and newspaper verse in the New York School of Journalism, where he succeeded Joyce Kilmer. Has contributed much humorous verse to *Life*. Now on the editorial staff of the *Literary Digest* and the *Woman's Home Companion*. His recent verse includes "The Laughing Muse," "A Ballad-Maker's Pack," and "The Light Guitar."

HAGEDORN, HERMANN (1882–   )

Born in New York. Author and editor. Formerly a member of the English faculty of Harvard; now interested in farming and the writing of novels, poems, plays, and biographies. Edited "Fifes and Drums," a collection of war poems, and has published five volumes of his own verse, besides "A Boy's Life of Roosevelt."

HARDY, THOMAS (1840–   )

English novelist and poet. Studied architecture, and was a prize-man in the Royal Institute of British Architects. Began his literary work as a poet, writing much verse from 1860 to 1870; then turned to prose, and produced a number of novels remarkable for their technique. In 1898 he returned to poetry, publishing "Wessex Poems," which he illustrated himself, and "The Dynasts," an epical drama of the Napoleonic wars. In 1919 his poetry was collected in his "Complete Poetical Works." He holds the gold medal of the Royal Society of Literature.

HENLEY, WILLIAM ERNEST (1849–1903)

English journalist, editor, writer of essays, plays, and vigorous, incisive poetry now published in his "Collected Poems." From boyhood he suffered from a tuberculous disease which necessitated the amputation of a foot. "In Hospital" pictures his life and surroundings at the infirmary in Edinburgh, where he met Robert Louis Stevenson, described in "Apparition"; while Stevenson used Henley as his model for John Silver in "Treasure Island."

HIGGINSON, ELLA RHOADS (Mrs. Russell C. Higginson) (1862–   )

Western writer of short stories, novels, books of travel, verse, and many popular songs. Was for several years the literary editor of the *Seattle Sunday Times*. Her "Message of Anne Laura Sweet" won the Collier $500 short-story prize in 1914.

HOUSMAN, ALFRED EDWARD (1859–   )

English writer; educated at St. John's College, Oxford. Was professor of Latin at University College, London, 1892–1911. Now Fellow of Trinity College and professor of Latin at Cambridge. A translator and author of papers for classical reviews. Published a volume of immortal lyrics, "A Shropshire Lad" (1896), but no more until "Last Poems" (1922).

HOUSMAN, LAURENCE (1865–   )

English artist and author, living in London. Brother of A. E. Housman. Well known for his essays in criticism, his stories, novels, and plays, as well as for his verse.

HOVEY, RICHARD (1864–1900)

Journalist, lecturer, translator, dramatist, and lyric poet. Was professor of English at Barnard College, New York. Collaborated with Bliss Carman in "Songs from Vagabondia" and "Along the Trail." Independently he wrote a group of remarkable poetic dramas based on the King Arthur legends.

HOYT, HELEN (Mrs. Jack Lyman)

Young poet, now living in the Middle West; contributor to many magazines. One of the associate editors of *Poetry: A Magazine of Verse*.

HUGHES, HUGH J.

Has written occasional verse. The events of his life are unknown.

HUGHES, RUPERT (1872–   )

Journalist, novelist, playwright, and writer of short stories. Served as a major in the World War. Two of his best-known works are "Excuse Me," a play produced in America, Europe, and Australia, and "The Old Nest," now filmed.

IRWIN, WALLACE (1876–   )

Author and editor. Has been connected with many newspapers and magazines in San Francisco, and later in New York. His latest publication is "The Seed of the Sun," a novel of life in California. Is widely known as a humorist and burlesque writer through his "Love Sonnets of a Hoodlum," "The Rubaiyat of Omar Khayyam, Jr.," and "The Blooming Angel."

JOHNSON, E. PAULINE (1862–1913)

Princess Tekahion'wake, an Indian writer, daughter of a head chief of the Mohawk tribe in Ontario, Canada. Wrote poems and prose sympathetic with nature and human nature. Recited her own poems widely throughout the United States and on the Pacific coast of Canada. Her poems are collected in "Flint and Feather," with an introduction by Theodore Watts-Dunton.

JONES, THOMAS SAMUEL, JR. (1882–   )

Began his literary work as a newspaper dramatic critic; was on the staff of the *New York Times*. Is now associate editor of the *Pathfinder*. Contributes poetry to the leading magazines. "The Rose-Jar" and "The Voice in the Silence" won for him high rank among the younger American writers both for theme and for expression.

KEMP, HARRY HIBBARD (1883–   )

Sometimes called the Tramp Poet, because he traveled around the world, starting from New York with twenty-five cents. Now lives in New York, where he has founded his own theater, in which he is actor, stage manager, playwright, and chorus. He also writes plays, novels, stories, and poems. "Chanteys and Ballads" is his latest and most representative book of verse.

KILMER, JOYCE (1886–1918)

Literary editor, journalist, and writer of essays and poems. America's best-known "Gold Star" poet, killed in action in the second battle of the Marne, while serving as sergeant. His poems, essays, and letters are now collected in one volume. His widow, Aline Kilmer, is also a poet.

KIPLING, RUDYARD (1865–   )

Great Britain's foremost man of letters. An untiring, fearless, and prophetic writer of both prose and poetry. Born in Bombay and educated in England, he returned to India to take up journalistic work at Lahore. His intimate knowledge of Anglo-Indian, Asiatic, and seafaring life is reflected in many dramatic and well-wrought tales, sketches, and ballads. Married an American, and lived in Vermont for several

years. In 1890 he returned to England, where, except when on long
travel tours, he has since resided, at first in London, recently in Sussex.
Kipling's latest work, "Irish Guards in the Great War" is in the nature
of a memorial to Lieutenant John Kipling, his only son, who was offi-
cially reported as "lost" in Belgium.

"Recessional" has been set to music by many composers; the best-
known setting is by Reginald de Koven.

LANG, ANDREW (1844–1912)

Journalist, historian, anthropologist, philologist, translator, critic,
and poet. Born in Selkirk, Scotland, and educated at Edinburgh
Academy, St. Andrews University, and Oxford. Was a lecturer at St.
Andrews from 1881 to 1912. A prolific writer in the field of criticism,
folklore, history, and poetry. Like Dobson, he was much interested in
Old French verse forms. He is well known as a translator of Homer's
Odyssey and Iliad and as the author of a "History of Scotland" in
four volumes.

LEDWIDGE, FRANCIS (1891–1917)

Young Irish poet who followed many occupations during his brief
but romantic life. Serving as a lance corporal, he was killed in action
on the Flanders front on July 19, 1917. His melodious, colorful poetry,
rich in nature images, has since been edited by Lord Dunsany, a
compatriot.

LE GALLIENNE, RICHARD (1866–   )

Born at Liverpool, and English by birth and education, but American by long residence. Followed a commercial life for seven years;
then became a man of letters. His writings include critical essays, biographies, and poetry, all strongly influenced by the æsthetic movement.
His poetry is delicate, fanciful, and marked by fine lyric passion.

LETTS, WINIFRED M. (1887–   )

An Irish writer, whose "Songs from Leinster" reflect the humor and
pathos of the peasants of her early surroundings in western Ireland.
Her experiences as a volunteer war nurse are embodied in "Poems of
the War." "The Spires of Oxford" is one of the most perfect lyrics
inspired by the World War.

LILLARD, R. W.

"America's Answer" was written immediately after the death of
Lieutenant-Colonel John McCrae, author of "In Flanders Fields," and
was first published in the *New York Evening Post* (1918).

LOVEMAN, ROBERT (1864–   )

Author of much lyric poetry, especially songs of the South. Has published several volumes. His "April Rain" is one of our best native songs.

LOWELL, AMY (1874–   )

A New England writer; a granddaughter of a cousin of James Russell Lowell; sister of Abbott Lawrence Lowell, president of Harvard University, and of the late Percival Lowell, the astronomer. Devoted eight years to the practice of writing poetry without publishing a word. Is America's foremost exponent of free verse, although her own six volumes of verse contain many standard forms. Is also the author of two comprehensive and valuable criticisms of poetry, "Six French Poets" and "Tendencies in Modern American Poetry."

MCCARTHY, DENIS ALOYSIUS (1870–   )

Poet and journalist, born in Ireland. Writer for Boston papers and Eastern magazines. Lecturer on literary, patriotic, and social topics, and reader of his own poems. His rhythmic verse, frequently in Irish dialect, includes "Songs from Erin" and "Songs of Sunrise" and several patriotic songs.

MCCRAE, JOHN (1872–1918)

Distinguished Canadian physician; graduate of Toronto University and medical lecturer at Johns Hopkins, Baltimore. Was member of the medical staff of McGill University, Montreal. Served in the Boer War, and continuously for three years during the World War. Died of pneumonia while in service, January, 1918. "In Flanders Fields and Other Poems," published posthumously, includes an interesting and illuminating essay on his poetry and character.

"In Flanders Fields," written during active service in the battle of the Marne, is probably the most widely read poem of the World War. It is a perfect rondeau, one of the strictest French verse forms.

MCGROARTY, JOHN STEVEN (1862–   )

A Pennsylvania author, resident since 1901 in California. Writer of essays, books of travel, sketches, and several volumes of poems. Is much interested in the romance of early California, especially its missions. His popular "Mission Play" and "La Golondrina" are dramatic presentations of this early history.

MACNAIR, J. H.

Author of "Animal Tales from Africa."

MALLOCH, DOUGLAS (1877–   )

Newspaper reporter and author; now associate editor of the *American Lumberman*. Was president of the American Press Humorists in 1918. Has written much verse relating to forest and lumber camps in his six volumes, the latest being "Come on Home" (1923).

MARKHAM, EDWIN (1852–   )

A native of Oregon who moved to California and made his name there as a poet, writer, and lecturer. Was principal of the Tompkins School in Oakland, California, when in 1899 he published "The Man with the Hoe," a poem which won world-wide attention. Has resided in New York since 1901. Besides his books and lectures on labor and child-labor problems, he has published several volumes of verse. Among them are "Songs of Happiness" and "Gates of Paradise."

MASEFIELD, JOHN (1874–   )

One of Great Britain's best-known writers. A poet, novelist, and dramatist. Lured by love of the sea and adventure, he shipped as a cabin boy and spent several years before the mast and in various lands. Returning to England in 1896, he devoted himself to literature. Much of his thrilling verse and narrative poetry reflects his love of the sea. During the World War he fitted out a hospital ship at his own expense, served with the Red Cross in France, was government historian for the Gallipoli campaign and the battle of the Somme, and made a lecture tour through the United States, mainly to the army camps. His versatile writings include much poetry, poetic plays, critical work, and several novels and stories for boys. His young daughter Judith has illustrated his last two books, "Right Royal" (a horse-racing story) and "King Cole." "August, 1914," almost the finest literary product of the war, is one of the great modern odes. It may well be compared to Gray's "Elegy in a Country Churchyard."

MIFFLIN, LLOYD (1846–1921)

Pennsylvania author and poet. Studied art in Europe but, because of poor health, turned to literature, writing much verse. Is a master of the sonnet form; over four hundred and fifty of high quality are published in his "Collected Sonnets."

MILLAY, EDNA ST. VINCENT (Mrs. Eugen Boissevain) (1892–   )

Young poet who gained immediate literary recognition through her first volume, "Renascence and Other Poems," which was soon followed by three other books of verse. Won the Columbia Prize for poetry in

1921 and the Pulitzer Prize for poetry in 1922. Her recent volumes are "A Few Figs from Thistles" and "The Harp-Weaver and Other Poems" (1923).

MORGAN, ANGELA

Began as a writer for Chicago, Boston, and New York papers. Also a lecturer and platform speaker. Author of much thoughtful, forward-looking, and incisive verse and fiction. At the Hague Conference in 1915 she read an original poem, "The Battle Cry of the Mothers." Her poem "To the Unknown Soldier" was recited in the rotunda of the Capitol at Washington on November 11, 1921. Her latest volume of verse is "The Luminous Heart"; the best known are "The Hour Has Struck" and "Hail, Man!"

MORLEY, CHRISTOPHER DARLINGTON (1890–)

Journalist, editor, and author. Was Rhodes Scholar at Oxford. Now editor of the literary "Bowling Green" column of the *New York Evening Post*. Writes plays, essays, fiction, and humorous, whimsical, imaginative poetry. "Chimneysmoke" is one of his late volumes of verse. "Plum Pudding" and "Where the Blue Begins" are other recent publications.

MORTON, DAVID (1886–)

Kentucky poet. Educated at Vanderbilt University, Nashville. Was in newspaper work for six years in Louisville; now a teacher, living in Morristown, New Jersey. Is on the editorial board of *The Measure*, a New York journal of poetry. Author of "Ships in Harbour," which contains many fine sonnets in the Shakespearean form.

NATHANSON, NATHANIEL

A writer of occasional verse. The events of his life are unknown.

NEWBOLT, SIR HENRY JOHN (1862–)

English lawyer and author. Is professor of poetry and was member of the Academic Committee (1911–1921) of the Royal Society of Literature. A great lover of the sea, he has written vigorous stories of sea life and many stirring sea songs and ballads. He has also written historical novels, tales of the World War, and essays on English poetry, and has published "An English Anthology." His "Songs of the Sea" and "Songs of the Fleet" have been set to music.

NOYES, ALFRED (1880–)

One of our foremost poets. Born in Staffordshire and educated at Oxford, where he was a winning crew man. Is well known in America as a lecturer on poetry and as a reader of his own poetry. Has been a professor of modern poetry for several years at Princeton University. During the World War he served in the British Foreign Office, and in 1919 was created C.B.E. (Commander of British Empire). Author of much melodious verse, ballads, epics, dramas, short stories, essays, and fiction. His magical "Tale of Old Japan" has been set to music as a cantata by Coleridge-Taylor.

O'SHEEL, SHAEMAS (1886–   )

New York writer who took the ancient Gaelic form of his family name, Shields. A follower of the Celtic revival movement, which has strongly influenced all his poetry in theme and mysticism. Author of "The Blossoming Bough" and "The Light Feet of Goats."

OXENHAM, JOHN

A native of Yorkshire. Educated at Manchester, England. Fond of Alpine climbing and of rowing. Formerly a business man in France and the United States. His first volume was published in 1898. Now a voluminous writer of essays, stories, and verse. In America the best known of his several volumes of poems is "The Vision Splendid"; his latest is "Gentlemen—The King!" (1920).

PAINE, ALBERT BIGELOW (1861–   )

Author and editor, formerly connected with *St. Nicholas Magazine*. Besides has published much fiction and some biography, notably a "Biography of Mark Twain" and "The Boys' Life of Mark Twain." One of his most recent publications is "The Car that went Abroad" (1921).

PALMER, ALICE FREEMAN (Mrs. George H. Palmer) (1855–1902)

A foremost pioneer educator of women in the United States. Was professor of history at Wellesley, and later its president. Afterwards was Dean of Women at the University of Chicago. Her biography by her husband, Professor George H. Palmer of Harvard University, gives a discriminating account of her life work.

PEABODY, JOSEPHINE PRESTON (Mrs. Lionel S. Marks) (1874–1922)

A writer of lyric and dramatic poetry; formerly an instructor at Wellesley. Married Professor L. S. Marks of Harvard University. Her artistic, imaginative play "The Piper" won the $10,000 Stratford-on-Avon Prize in 1910.

PECK, SAMUEL MINTURN (1854–   )

Southern writer; born, educated, and now residing in Alabama. First contributed poems to newspapers and magazines while he was studying medicine in New York. Has published six volumes of verse, mainly lyric, besides short stories, novels, and articles for periodicals. Is well known for his "Grapevine Swing" and a Yale College song, "The Knot of Blue."

PERCY, WILLIAM ALEXANDER (1885–   )

A Southern lawyer and poet. Born in Greenville, Mississippi; graduate of Harvard; has practiced in Greenville since 1908. During the World War he served as captain in the A.E.F. in France. Author of "Sappho in Levkas" and "In April Once."

PHILLPOTTS, EDEN (1862–   )

An English novelist of Devonshire stock born in India. Studied for the stage, but abandoned it for literature, to which he has devoted himself, writing short stories, plays, and poems, in addition to a great number of novels, especially of life in Dartmoor, in the West Country. "As the Wind Blows" is his latest book of verse.

PICKTHALL, MARJORIE L. C. (1888–1922)

Novelist and poet; born in London, England, but came to Canada at an early age and became in sympathy and outlook essentially Canadian. Was visiting in England when the World War began and remained there all through the war, working on the land and serving as a groom-gardener. Published her first novel, "Little Hearts," in 1916, followed by "The Bridge" (a story of Toronto Island), in 1920, and a drama, "The Wood-Carver's Wife," staged in Canada in 1921 by the Community Players. She also wrote short stories for London and New York magazines. Has published two books of verse, "The Drift of Pinions" and "The Land of Poor Souls."

POOLE, LOUELLA C. (Mrs. Julius Pähtz)

New England writer of verse. Contributor to Eastern papers and magazines. Is especially interested in the protection of dumb animals, and writes much verse for humane societies.

POWELL, ARTHUR

Young poet; a frequent contributor to magazines.

PRATT, HARRY NOYES (1879–   )

Poet, art critic, and lecturer on verse. Born in Wisconsin, but has resided in California since 1903. Author of "Hill Trails and Open Sky." Winner of the Laura Blackburn Lyric Poetry Prize in 1922 and 1923.

RAWNSLEY, HARDWICKE DRUMMOND (1851–1920)

English clergyman and religious writer. Was canon of Carlisle and honorary chaplain to the king. Edited many books and guidebooks on the local history of the English Lake Country and its traditions. His verse includes "Sonnets" and "Poems at Home and Abroad."

REESE, LIZETTE WOODWORTH (1856–   )

Teacher of English in the West High School in Baltimore. Author of six volumes of lyric verse: "A Branch of May," "A Handful of Lavender," "A Quiet Road," "A Wayside Lute," "Spicewood," and "Wild Cherry" (1923), all as charming as their titles.

RILEY, JAMES WHITCOMB (1853–1916)

One of America's popular poets. Began writing as a newspaper man. His popularity is due largely to the simplicity of his themes and his sympathetic appeal to readers of all classes. Well known as the "Hoosier Poet" because much of his verse is written in Middle Western dialect. His birthday, October 7, "Riley Day," is now celebrated annually in his own state, Indiana. His voluminous verse is collected in a complete biographical edition.

RITTENHOUSE, JESSIE BELLE (Mrs. Bliss Carman) (1869–   )

New York author and critic. Now a contributor to newspaper and press syndicates and a lecturer on modern poetry at Columbia University. Editor of three anthologies of American poetry; author of a book of critical essays, "The Younger American Poets," and two volumes of poems, "The Door of Dreams" and "The Lifted Cup."

ROBERTSON, JAMES LOGIE (pen name, "Hugh Haliburton") (1850–1922)

Educator, editor, poet, novelist, critic, and student of geology. Born in Kinross-shire, Scotland, and educated at Edinburgh University. Head English master at Edinburgh Ladies College from 1891 to 1914, when he retired. Has published, among other works, "Poems," "Excursions in Prose and Verse," "Nature in Books," a "History of Scottish Literature," and critical works on English men of letters.

ROBINSON, CORINNE ROOSEVELT (Mrs. Douglas Robinson) (1861–   )

Younger sister of Theodore Roosevelt, whose biography she has written. Very active in Red Cross work, charities, and civic activities and organizations. Is also the author of three volumes of verse.

ROBINSON, EDWIN ARLINGTON (1869–   )

One of America's foremost poets. Born in High Tide, Maine. Struggled to make a living in various capacities until Theodore Roosevelt, recognizing his literary genius as exhibited in "Captain Craig," gave him a position in the New York customs office. His first volume was published in 1897. Among his important writings are "The Man against the Sky," "Merlin," and "Launcelot and Guinevere" which won the Lyric Society Prize in 1919. "Collected Poems" was also awarded a prize in 1921, and he was further signally honored in 1922 by a commemorative essay by the Poetic Society of America. His verse is distinguished by its flawless technique, his unerring choice of words, his mastery of blank verse, his sure grasp of the central thought and a definite philosophy, amounting, in "The Man against the Sky," to a real interpretation of life. For these achievements he has been a distinct formative influence in modern poetry.

SANDBURG, CARL (1878–   )

Chicago journalist and editorial writer. After following many occupations he became a reporter, then a magazine and newspaper editor. Has published four volumes of free verse, mainly portraying industrial American life. The most discussed was "Chicago Poems"; the most recent is "Slabs of the Sunburnt West."

SANTAYANA, GEORGE (1863–   )

Born in Madrid, Spain. Came to America when eight years old; resident of New York. Was professor of philosophy at Harvard University. Besides essays and poetry, he has written many important books on philosophical subjects. His sonnets are especially fine; he has a classic mastery of this form of poetry. His latest publications are "Soliloquies in England," a series of entertaining essays (1922), and "Later Soliloquies." A fine selection of his poems has recently been issued (1923).

SCHAUFFLER, ROBERT HAVEN (1879–   )

An American author; a descendant of several generations of American ancestors, despite his foreign name and Austrian birthplace. Is a cellist of reputation and an amateur sculptor; was the winner of the national tennis championship (doubles) in Rome in 1906; was an army officer during the World War. Well known as a lecturer and a writer of essays and poems, especially on travel and musical subjects. Among his recent volumes are "Fiddler's Luck" and "Magic Flame" (1923).

SCOLLARD, CLINTON (1860–   )

Author and editor, now living in New York City. Was professor of English literature at Hamilton College, New York. Has published many volumes of lyric verse. Among his recent ones are "The Vale of

Shadows and Other Verses of the Great War," "Italy in Arms and Other Verses," and "The Epic of Golf."

SEEGER, ALAN (1886–1916)

Gifted young American "Gold Star" poet. Graduated from Harvard, and went to Paris in 1912 as student and writer. At the outbreak of the war in August, 1914, he enlisted in the Foreign Legion of France and served exultantly until his death on July 5, 1916, in an attack on Belloy-en-Santerre. "Poems" contains his collected verse, with a biographical introduction by William Archer. "I have a Rendezvous with Death," one of the gems of literature inspired by the war, is probably the finest poem written by a soldier in actual service. Seeger, like Brooke, "loved life tremendously, and gave it up unhesitatingly."

SHERMAN, FRANK DEMPSTER (1860–1916)

Was professor of graphics at Columbia School of Architecture. A writer of lyrics, a genealogist, and a designer, especially of book plates. Published four volumes of lyrics, the last "A Southern Flight," in collaboration with Clinton Scollard, who wrote the introduction to the collected edition of Sherman's poems.

SMITH, CICELY FOX (1882–   )

An English writer, a lineal descendant of Captain John Smith of Virginia; lives in London. She spent several years on the Pacific coast of Canada to satisfy her love of the sea and of ships. Her publications include three novels with Canadian setting; two volumes of vigorous sea songs and ballads, "Sailor Town" and "Small Craft"; and "Fighting Men," a collection of her war verse.

SPEYER, LADY LEONORA (von Stosch) (1872–   )

A poet who contributes lyric verse to many magazines; also a lecturer on poetry and music. Born, educated, and resides in Washington, D.C. Was a professional violinist before her marriage to Sir Edgar Speyer. Has recently published "A Canopic Jar," a volume of verse.

STANTON, FRANK LEBBY (1857–   )

Journalist and verse writer, identified with the Atlanta press for many years. Now on the staff of the *Atlanta Constitution*. Well known as a public reader of his own poems, which are mainly lyrics of the South.

STEPHENS, JAMES (1882–   )

Irish poet and novelist. One of the most gifted of the modern school of Irish writers. Now Assistant Director of the National Gallery

of Ireland as an authority on art. Was a typist and shorthand clerk
in a lawyer's office in Dublin when his writings attracted the attention
of "A. E." (George W. Russell). He knows Ireland and its people intimately. He is a spirited writer of imaginative verse, especially of Irish
character. Gained sudden fame in 1912 by his story "The Crock of
Gold," and has since published five volumes of poems marked by a
quaint and original blending of humor, realism, and fantasy.

STOLTZE, JOHN

A graduate of Princeton University, 1917.

TEASDALE, SARA (Mrs. Ernst B. Filsinger) (1884–   )

A lyric poet, now living in New York City. Her volume of "Love
Songs" received the Columbia Prize of $500 for the best book of verse
in 1917. "Flame and Shadow," the latest of her five volumes, contains
several songs of exquisite beauty. Edited "The Answering Voice," an
anthology of love lyrics by women.

THOMAS, EDITH MATILDA (1854–   )

One of America's accomplished veteran women writers, now living
in New York. Was on the editorial staff of *Harper's Magazine*. An
editor and poet who has written many excellent lyrics, published in ten
volumes.

THOMPSON, FRANCIS (1860–1907)

Talented English poet and contributor to critical reviews. Educated
for medicine, but left home in Manchester when seventeen and went to
London, where he tried many strange ways of earning a living. Living
in terrible poverty, which had undermined his health, he was discovered
and cared for by an appreciative editor, Wilfred Meynell, who published his verse. His impassioned life flamed with religious fervor, at
its height in his masterpiece "The Hound of Heaven."

TOVEY, DUNCAN

Writer of occasional verse. The events of his life are unknown.

TOWNE, CHARLES HANSON (1877–   )

Journalist and magazine editor in New York City. Was formerly
editor of the *Designer* and *Smart Set*; now the managing editor of
McClure's Magazine. Author of much prose, several volumes of verse,
two books for children, and the words for many songs and some operas.
Over a hundred and fifty of his songs have been set to music by famous
composers. Well known in New York for his geniality and as a

creator of witty epigrams. Has recently published "Loafing down Long Island," a series of sketches, and a novel, "The Gay Ones" (1924).

TURNER, NANCY BYRD

Contributor of verse to leading periodicals and magazines. Has recently published a book of juvenile poems, "Zodiac Town."

TYNAN, KATHARINE (Mrs. H. A. Hinkson) (1861–   )

Irish novelist and poet whose first volume of verse appeared in 1885. Reviews Irish literature for the London *Bookman*. Author of much prose, of several plays, and many ballads, lyrics, and religious poems. Her verse in dialect is her most characteristic and best work.

UNTERMEYER, LOUIS (1885–   )

A New York jeweler and designer by profession. A lecturer on poetry, a translator, parodist, and reviewer of verse, as well as a writer of poetry. Has edited anthologies of both British and American modern poetry, and "This Singing World," an anthology for children. His best work of criticism is "The New Era in Contemporary Poetry."

UPTON, MINNIE LEONA

An Eastern writer. A frequent contributor of verse to *St. Nicholas Magazine*.

VAN DYKE, HENRY (1852–   )

Author and diplomat. A Presbyterian minister, and Moderator of the General Assembly, 1902–1903. Professor of English at Princeton since 1900. Oxford conferred the highest academic degree, Doctor of Civil Law, upon him in 1917. Was American minister to the Netherlands and Luxemburg from June, 1913, to December, 1916, and has recorded his diplomatic experiences in "Fighting for Peace." Has written many volumes of prose and verse, especially nature poems, and edited many books on English poetry.

WALTER, HOWARD ARNOLD (1883–1918)

Missionary. Was teacher of English in Tokyo, Japan; afterwards assistant pastor in Hartford, Connecticut. Was secretary of the International Committee of the Y.M.C.A. Went to Lahore, India, as secretary of the Foreign Missionary League for India and the Far East. Author of poems and religious works, especially relating to India.

WATSON, ROSAMUND MARRIOTT (Mrs. William H. Watson) (1863–1911)

English writer of lyrics. Was the wife of William H. Watson, the well-known English author and editor. At her best in nature poems.

The most representative of her five volumes of verse is "A Summer Night"; her best poem is "Resurgam."

WEIR, ARTHUR (1864–1902)

Canadian journalist and poet. Born and educated in Montreal, he became a journalist on the *Montreal Star* and *The Journal of America*. Has published considerable prose and three volumes of verse.

WHEELOCK, JOHN HALL (1886–)

Editor and poet; manager of the library department of Charles Scribner's Sons. Compiled the poems and wrote the biography for Alan Seeger's "Poems and Letters." Has contributed much poetry to magazines and has published four volumes of verse, including "The Beloved Adventure" and "Dust and Light." Has recently published "A Biography of Roosevelt."

WIDDEMER, MARGARET (Mrs. Robert Haven Schauffler)

New York poet, novelist, writer of short stories, and juvenile books. Has published three books of verse, "The Factories and Other Poems," "The Old Road to Paradise," and "Cross Currents," and an anthology of ghost poems, "The Haunted Hour."

WILKINSON, MARGUERITE O. BIGELOW (Mrs. James G. Wilkinson) (1883–)

A native of Halifax, Nova Scotia, but educated at Evanston, Illinois. Now a resident of New York. Writer of plays, essays, and lyrics lecturer on contemporary poetry; a discriminating critic; compiler of "New Voices," a modern American anthology. Her own writings include "In Vivid Gardens," "Bluestone," and "The Dingbat of Arcady." The Introduction to "Bluestone" contains an interesting discussion of the relation of music to poetry. The author analyzes the verse structure of "A Chant Out of Doors" as a mood of worship alternating with a mood of wonder.

WOODS, CHARLES COKE (1860–)

Minister and author. Born in Illinois, and educated at Northwestern University, Chicago. Lived for sixteen years in Kansas, where he is well known as a speaker and writer. Now a pastor in Monrovia, California. Two of his books, "In the Beauty of Meadow and Mountain" and "The Old Home," are illustrated by his wife.

YEATS, WILLIAM BUTLER (1865–)

Irish poet and playwright. Spent his childhood at Sligo, where he learned the fairy stories, native folklore, and tales of the Irish peasants.

Studied art, but followed literature. One of the leaders in the Celtic revival. With Lady Gregory he founded the Abbey Theater, Dublin, to promote national independence in the drama. Has lectured and read from his own verse in America. Has written symbolic plays of haunting spirituality, notably "The Hour Glass" and "The Land of Heart's Desire." His poetic work, frequently Irish in theme and phrasing, is characterized by its magical beauty and elusiveness. He was awarded the Nobel Prize for Literature in 1923.

BIBLIOGRAPHY

CRITICISM OF CONTEMPORARY POETRY

AIKEN, CONRAD P. Scepticisms : Notes on Contemporary Poetry.
Alfred A. Knopf, Inc., 1919.

BOYNTON, PERCY H. American Poetry. Charles Scribner's Sons,
1918.

BOYNTON, PERCY H. A History of American Literature. Ginn
and Company, 1919.

COOK, HOWARD WILLARD. Our Poets of Today. Moffat, Yard,
and Company, 1918.

CUNLIFFE, J. WILLIAM, and LOMER, G. R. English Literature
during the Last Half Century. The Century Co., 1922.

EASTMAN, MAX. Enjoyment of Poetry. Charles Scribner's Sons,
1913.

GARVIN, JOHN WILLIAM. Canadian Poets and Poetry. Frederick A.
Stokes Company, 1917.

GRAVES, R. On English Poetry. Alfred A. Knopf, Inc., 1922.

HIND, CHARLES LEWIS. Authors and I. J. Lane, 1921.

HIND, CHARLES LEWIS. More Authors and I. J. Lane, 1922.

HUBBELL, J. B., and BEATY, JOHN O. An Introduction to Poetry.
The Macmillan Company, 1922.

KERNAHAN, COULSON. Five Famous Living Poets. Thornton
Butterworth.

LONG, WILLIAM J. American Literature (1923 edition). Ginn
and Company.

LONG, WILLIAM J. English Literature (1923 edition). Ginn and
Company.

LOWELL, AMY. Tendencies in Modern American Poetry. The
Macmillan Company, 1917.

LOWES, JOHN LIVINGSTON. Convention and Revolt in Poetry. Houghton Mifflin Company, 1919.

MANLY, JOHN M., and RICKERT, EDITH. Contemporary American Literature. Harcourt, Brace and Company, Inc., 1921.

MANLY, JOHN M., and RICKERT, EDITH. Contemporary British Literature. Harcourt, Brace and Company, Inc., 1921.

MAYNARD, THEODORE. Our Best Poets, English and American. Henry Holt and Company, 1922.

NEWBOLT, HENRY JOHN. A New Study of English Poetry. E. P. Dutton & Company, 1919.

PERRY, BLISS. A Study of Poetry. Houghton Mifflin Company, 1920.

PHELPS, WILLIAM LYON. The Advance of Poetry in the Twentieth Century. Dodd, Mead & Company, 1918.

RICH, MABEL IRENE. A Study of the Types in Literature. The Century Co., 1921.

RITTENHOUSE, JESSIE B. Younger American Poets. Little, Brown & Company, 1904.

ROTHERSTEIN, WILLIAM. Twenty-four Portraits. Harcourt, Brace and Company, Inc., 1921.

STURGEON, MARY C. Studies in Contemporary Poets. Dodd, Mead & Company, 1920.

UNTERMEYER, LOUIS. A New Era in American Poetry. Henry Holt and Company, 1919.

WILKINSON, MARGUERITE. New Voices. The Macmillan Company, 1919.

WILLIAMS, HAROLD. Modern English Poetry. Alfred A. Knopf, Inc., 1919.

WOODBERRY, GEORGE EDWARD. A New Defense of Poetry (in "The Heart of Man"). Harcourt, Brace and Company, Inc., 1920.

WOODBERRY, GEORGE EDWARD. An Appreciation of Literature. Harcourt, Brace and Company, Inc., 1922.

COLLECTIONS CONTAINING CONTEMPORARY VERSE

American Poetry: a Miscellany. Harcourt, Brace and Company, Inc., 1920.

ANDREWS, C. E. From the Front. D. Appleton and Company, 1918.

Anthology of American Humor in Verse. Duffield & Company, 1917.

BOYNTON, PERCY H. Milestones in American Literature. Ginn and Company, 1923.

BRAITHWAITE, WILLIAM STANLEY. Anthology of Magazine Verse. Small, Maynard and Company, yearly since 1914.

BRAITHWAITE, WILLIAM STANLEY. Poetic Year for 1916. Small, Maynard and Company, 1916.

BRAITHWAITE, WILLIAM STANLEY. Golden Treasury of Magazine Verse. Small, Maynard and Company, 1918.

BRAITHWAITE, WILLIAM STANLEY. Book of Modern British Verse. Small, Maynard and Company, 1919.

BROADHURST, JEAN, and RHOADES, CLARA LAWTON. Verse for Patriots. J. B. Lippincott Company, 1919.

BROWNE, WALDO R. Joys of the Road. Atlantic Monthly Press, 1923.

CALDWELL, T. The Golden Book of Modern Verse. E. P. Dutton & Company, 1922.

CAMPBELL, WILFRID. The Oxford Book of Canadian Verse. Oxford University Press, 1914.

CLARKE, GEORGE HERBERT. A Treasury of War Poetry. Houghton Mifflin Company, First Series, 1918; Second Series, 1919.

CLAUSON, J. E. A Dog's Book of Verse. Small, Maynard and Company, 1916.

COLUM, PADRAIC. Anthology of Irish Verse. Boni & Liveright, 1922.

CONSTABLE, JOHN. Some Imagist Poetry. Houghton Mifflin Company. Vol. I, 1915; Vol. II, 1916; Vol. III, 1917.

CRABB, W. Poems of the Golden West. Harr Wagner Publishing Co.

CUNLIFFE, JOHN WILLIAM. Poems of the Great War. The Macmillan Company, 1919.

DAVIS, M. G. Girls' Book of Verse. Frederick A. Stokes Company, 1922.

DE LA MARE, WALTER. Come Hither; A Collection of Poems for Children. Harcourt, Brace and Company, Inc., 1923.

DRINKWATER, JOHN. The Way of Poetry. Houghton Mifflin Company, 1922.

EARLE, FERDINAND. The Lyric Year. Mitchell Kennerley, 1912.

EDGAR, W. C. The Bellman Book of Verse, 1906–1919. The Bellman Co., 1919.

FARRAR, JOHN. The Bookman Anthology of Verse. George H. Doran Company, 1922.

FISH, H. W. Book of New York Verse. G. P. Putnam's Sons, 1917.

FOXCROFT, FRANK. War Verse. Thomas Y. Crowell Company, 1918.

FROTHINGHAM, ROBERT. Songs of Men. Houghton Mifflin Company, 1918.

FROTHINGHAM, ROBERT. Songs of Dogs. Houghton Mifflin Company, 1920.

FROTHINGHAM, ROBERT. Songs of Horses. Houghton Mifflin Company, 1920.

FROTHINGHAM, ROBERT. Songs of Challenge. Houghton Mifflin Company, 1922.

GARVIN, JOHN WILLIAM. Canadian Poems of the Great War. McClelland & Stewart, 1918.

Georgian Poetry: 1911–1912; 1913–1915; 1916–1917; 1918–1919; 1919–1920. Poetry Bookshop, London.

GIBBONS, HERBERT ADAMS. Songs from the Trenches. Harper & Brothers, 1918.

GORDON, MARGERY, and KING, MARIE B. Verse of Our Day. D. Appleton and Company, 1923.

GRAHAM, P. A. Country Life Anthology of Verse. Charles Scribner's Sons, 1915.

GRAVES, A. P. Book of Irish Poetry. Frederick A. Stokes Company, 1915.

HAYNES, WILLIAM, and HARRISON, J. L. Fisherman's Verse. Duffield & Company, 1919.

HEFFLER. Cambridge Poets, 1910–1913; 1914–1920. Cambridge University Press.

JOHNSON, JAMES WELDON. Book of American Negro Poetry. Harcourt, Brace and Company, Inc., 1922.

LE GALLIENNE, RICHARD. Modern Book of American Verse. Boni & Liveright, 1919.

LE GALLIENNE, RICHARD. Book of English Verse. Boni & Liveright, 1922.

LOMAX, JOHN. Cowboy Songs and Other Frontier Ballads. The Macmillan Company, 1919.

LOMAX, JOHN. Songs of the Cattle Trail and Cow Camp. The Macmillan Company, 1919.

LUCAS, EDWARD VERRALL. The Open Road. Henry Holt and Company, 1913.

MASSINGHAM, HAROLD JOHN. Poems about Birds. E. P. Dutton & Company, 1922.

MATTHEWS, BRANDER. Poems of American Patriotism (Revised). Charles Scribner's Sons, 1922.

METHUEN, A. An Anthology of Modern Verse. Methuen & Co., London, 1921.

MONROE, HARRIET, and HENDERSON, ALICE C. The New Poetry: An Anthology. The Macmillan Company, 1917; Revised, 1920.

MOORE, T. S. Some Soldier Poets. Harcourt, Brace and Company, Inc., 1920.

MORRIS, JOSEPH, and ADAMS, ST. CLAIR. Songs for Fishermen. Stewart Kidd, Publishers, 1922.

MURDOCK, W. Oxford Book of Australian Verse. Oxford University Press, 1919.

NEWBOLT, HENRY JOHN. Anthology of English Literature. E. P. Dutton & Company, 1919.

NICHOLSON, D. H. S., and LEE, A. H. E. The Oxford Book of English Mystical Verse. Oxford University Press, 1917.

NOYES, ALFRED. Princeton Book of Verse. Princeton University Press, 1916.

O'BRIEN, EDWARD J. The Masque of Poets. Dodd, Mead & Company, 1918.

OSBORN, EDWARD BOLLAND. The Muse in Arms. Frederick A. Stokes Company, 1918.

OSBORN, EDWARD BOLLAND. New Elizabethans. John Lane Company, 1919.

Oxford Poetry, 1910–1914; 1914–1916; 1918; 1919; 1920. Oxford University Press.

PALGRAVE, FRANCIS. Golden Treasury. The Macmillan Company, 1911; Revised, 1919.

PALGRAVE, FRANCIS. Golden Treasury of Songs and Lyrics. Scott, Foresman and Company, 1919.

POCOCK, GUY N. Modern Poetry (King's Treasuries of Literature). E. P. Dutton & Company, 1920.

PRESLAND, JOHN (Mrs. Gladys Skelton). Poems of London. The Macmillan Company, London, 1918.

Punch, London. Poems from *Punch*, 1909–1920. The Macmillan Company, 1922.

QUILLER-COUCH, ARTHUR T. The Oxford Book of English Verse. Oxford University Press, 1919.

RAND, THEODORE H. Treasury of Canadian Verse. Briggs and Company, 1910.

RICE, WALLACE, and RICE, FRANCES. The Humbler Poets: Magazine Verse. A. C. McClurg & Co., 1911.

RICHARDS, Mrs. WALDO (Gertrude E. Moore). High Tide. Houghton Mifflin Company, 1916.

RICHARDS, Mrs. WALDO (Gertrude E. Moore). Melody of Earth. Houghton Mifflin Company, 1918.

RICHARDS, Mrs. WALDO (Gertrude E. Moore). Star Points. Houghton Mifflin Company, 1921.

RICKERT, EDITH, and PATON, JESSIE. American Lyrics. Doubleday, Page & Company, 1912.

RITTENHOUSE, JESSIE B. The Little Book of Modern Verse. Houghton Mifflin Company, 1913.

RITTENHOUSE, JESSIE B. Little Book of American Poets. Houghton Mifflin Company, 1917.

RITTENHOUSE, JESSIE B. The Second Book of Modern Verse. Houghton Mifflin Company, 1919.

SEYMOUR, WILLIAM KEAN. Miscellany of British Poetry. Harcourt, Brace and Company, Inc., 1920.

SHELBY, ANNIE BLANCHE. The Lullaby Book. Duffield & Company, 1921.

Soldier Poets: Songs of the Fighting Men. Brentano's, 1919.

Soldier Poets: More Songs of the Fighting Men. Brentano's, 1919.

SQUIRE, JOHN COLLINGS. Book of Women's Verse. Oxford University Press, 1921.

SQUIRE, JOHN COLLINGS. Collected Parodies. George H. Doran Company, 1922.

SQUIRE, JOHN COLLINGS. Selections from Modern Poets. Martin Secker, London, 1922.

Stanford Book of Verse, 1912–1916. English Club, Stanford University.

STEVENSON, BURTON E. Home Book of Verse. Henry Holt and Company, Revised, 1918.

STORK, CHARLES WHARTON. Contemporary Verse Anthology, 1916–1920. E. P. Dutton & Company, 1920.

TEASDALE, SARA. The Answering Voice. Houghton Mifflin Company, 1917.

UNTERMEYER, LOUIS. Modern British Poetry. Harcourt, Brace and Company, Inc., 1920.

UNTERMEYER, LOUIS. Modern American Poetry. Harcourt, Brace and Company, Inc., 1921.

UNTERMEYER, LOUIS. Modern American and British Poetry. Harcourt, Brace and Company, Inc., 1922.

VAN DYKE, HENRY, and others. Princeton Book of Verse, Vol. II. Princeton University Press, 1919.

WALTERS, L. D'O. Anthology of Recent Poetry. Dodd, Mead & Company, 1920.

WALTERS, L. D'O. Irish Poets of To-day. E. P. Dutton & Company, 1921.

WARD, THOMAS HUMPHREY. The English Poets. Vol. V, Browning to Brooke. The Macmillan Company, 1918.

WELLS, CAROLYN. The Book of Humorous Verse. George H. Doran Company, 1920.

WHEELER, WILLIAM REGINALD. Book of Verse of the Great War. Yale University Press, 1917.

WIDDEMER, MARGARET. Haunted Hour: An Anthology. Harcourt, Brace and Company, Inc., 1920.

WILKINSON, MARGUERITE. Contemporary Poetry. The Macmillan Company, 1923.

WILKINSON, MARGUERITE. Golden Songs of the Golden State. A. C. McClurg & Co., 1917.

Yale Book of Student Verse, 1910–1919. Yale University Press, 1919.

Yale Review. American and British Verse from the *Yale Review.* Yale University Press, 1920.

INDEX TO FIRST LINES

PAGE

ALPHABETICAL INDEX OF TITLES

INDEX OF AUTHORS

Date Due

MAR 19 '45	AG 15 47	NOV 6 50	AUG 14 '70
APR 17 '45	NO 15 47	NOV 21 50	JAN 27 '72
DEC 4 45	DE 3 47	JAN 30 '51	MAY 10 74
FEB 20 '40		MAR 5 51	OCT 29 '75
OCT 8 46	DE 4 47	MR 3 '51	FEB 24 '77
OCT 22 46	JA 27 48	JUN 8 '53	APR 26 '82
OCT 29 46	FE 14 48	FEB 5 '54	
NOV 7 46	MR 10 48	MAY 26 '55	
NOV 23 46	JY 23 48	JUN - 4 '56	
NOV 25 48	AG 17 48	MAY 29 '57	
FEB 21 '47	DEC 4 48	MAY 1 5 '59	
MAR 00	DEC 8 48	OCT 3 1 '61	
MAR 13	MR 3 49	NOV 1 7 '61	
AP 1 '47	APR 25 49	MAR 1 0 '65	
AP 24 47	MAY 31 49	MAY 1 3 '65	
MY 20 47	FEB 17 50	JUN 2 5 '65	
	MAR 9 50	MAY 28 '66	
JY 31 47	MAR 9 '50	APR 9 '68	
	MAY 27 50		